Innovative Teaching, Learning & Evaluation in English

Innovative Teaching, Learning & Evaluation in English:

Harmonious Transition from School to University

(A Book on Proceedings of the UGC Sponsored International Seminar)

Editor

Pratyush Vatsala
Principal & Professor
Lakshmibai College
Univ. of Delhi

GYAN

ISBN: 978-81-212-2001-9

Published, 2020
Published by

Gyan Publishing House
5, Ansari Road
Daryaganj, New Delhi-110002
Phone: 011-47034999, 9811692060
www.gyanbooks.com
E-mail: books@gyanbooks.com

Printed at: G. Print Process, Delhi.

Contents

Acknowledgement

We thank the University Grants Commission and Trinity College London for sponsoring this International Seminar & Workshop. The UGC has also provided us support for publishing the Proceedings of the International Seminar on Innovative Teaching, Learning and Evaluation in English: Harmonious Transition from School to University which was held on 23, 24 & 25 January, 2020. We thank our esteemed guests and participants for sharing their thoughts during three day event. We are also grateful to our paper presenters who made meaningful contribution to the seminar and made this seminar a great success. The Department of English Lakshmibai College deserves applause for the successful academic endeavour.

Preface

The Board examination results have recently initiated a serious debate on our evaluation system. It is not CBSE or ICSE, Universities or Colleges, the education system is under scanner. If we deliberate on the issue of evaluation, the first thing that comes to our mind is fairness and objectivity of examination which must be ensured. But, in the name of objectivity in examination process, what we are doing is quite unfair to the youth. We have created a mechanism for input, output and delete options to be religiously followed by the students, crushing their creative spirit and the ability of critical thinking. Consequently, the students, incapable of critical thinking, turn critical about everything in the country. We do not train them in the art of criticism which is actually a discipline in which one needs a proper training. Being part of a generation with many avenues, options and distractions, our young students do not have time to pause for a while and think over what they are actually doing. The education system is miserably failing, if we are unable to tap the potential of our young minds and leaving them frustrated, despite their hard work and the achievements.

We need to rethink, if we are seriously preparing many achievers or just making a fool of ourselves and the youth or only promoting the business of coaching centres. The high score card does not promise them a happy life or even guarantees an admission to a University of their choice. We know that the score card without functional attributes, remains as a mere paper and the poor life skills attained during years of schooling and graduation make them more incapable of handling real life challenges and sometimes lead to suicides. This is not encouraging for Indian youth to study and grow in a time which is out of joint for various reasons and education is unable to help them setting it right for a meaningful existence. We need to really ponder over such questions and ensure that the evaluation system is capable of assessing knowledge and ability of students to understand, enabling them to apply the knowledge to real life situations and adding value to the life teaching then problem solving skills for a better life.

We, the teachers and students together owe the responsibility to make this world a better place to live, not only with the help of material achievements and advancements but also with emotional and spiritual growth, to contribute to the sustainable development of the world for the generations to come. The present education system is creating a mechanical version of students, scoring high grades but lacking in conceptual knowledge. We know that a machine has its own limitation and it is always a human mind that actually functions and performs behind a machine. Infact, the practical, critical, moral and creative aspects are missing from the content and delivery of learning material. Our students are talented but the evaluation system uses a generalised yardstick which does not have the unconventional parameters to assess their creativity and uniqueness. It is high time to correct our mistakes and save our future generation from despair. Learning from past experiences, we need to relook, reshape and recharge the system to enable us to educate and prepare our children in the real sense, so that they can understand true meaning of existence and find real happiness in life.

The education system we inherited from our ancient Bharat, never aimed at only cognitive development but it facilitated the holistic growth of the individual. It has always been a journey from being to becoming, from physical development to mental, social and spiritual development, integrating body, mind and soul. Thus, the aim of education with respect to our country is to impart that integral education to our young minds which is capable of character building.

Today, we need an education system which can have a harmonious blending of traditional and modern knowledge attributes and skill sets to fare through the 21st century challenges of the world in general and India, in particular. In view of this fact, the learning objectives and outcomes can be focused without confusion and the education system may be tweaked around these objectives as given in Delors Report 1996 as four pillars of learning, i.e. learning to know, learning to do, learning to live together and learning to be. These objectives of education are in sync with the Indian concept of Purusharthas promoting human values and higher attributes among mankind. A noble citizen, a compassionate human being, well aware of his/her social and environmental responsibility can be groomed, provided we can create an educational environment where joyful learning experience is dovetailed with the concept of development and growth at all five levels (Panchkoshas) of human existence. The ultimate aim is to learn, to discover, to realize and to manifest the inner potential.

India, that is Bharat has always assimilated the good, coming from all quarters, "Ano Bhadra Kratvo yantu Vishvatah". The resilience of Indian culture is exemplary. It has taken advantage of any crisis that it had to encounter. Gandhi also believed that we must keep the doors and windows of our mind open but not be swept away by the winds that we allowed to come in. We should never forget that our country has been through lots of ups and downs, still, it maintains a unique identity and character, rising every time with much more strength. The Sanjeevani comes from within. We have Hanumans and Sushen Vaidyas who guide us during any crisis or challenge. The truth, consciousness and bliss enshrined in our knowledge system and tradition help us to attain and maintain our real identity.

The real challenge is to adopt the technological advancements and yet preserve our value system. The question, how intellectual quotient can be aligned with the emotional and spiritual quotient and how it can be further aligned with 21st century skills and competencies along with the knowledge base acquired during be tailored to the competencies that equip for life with unification of sensibilities. The expansive outlook presented in the draft NEP 2019, UGC LOCF and UGC Evaluation Reforms further strengthens the vision of multifaceted development of the learner/ student to provide sustainable livelihoods and enlightenment of the individual.

The papers in the present volume focus on 21st Century skills, cooperative learning, Education 2.0, learning methodologies, reading skills and innovative practices, inculcating culture, soft skills and human values through English language and literature, language patterns and reflective state of happiness, shifting from quantitative assessment to qualitative assessments, going beyond the textbook, teaching first generation learners, setting benchmarks for teaching, learning and assessment picked up from the deliberations held during the International Seminar held in collaboration with Trinity College London on the theme of Innovative Teaching, Learning and Evaluation in English for a harmonious transition from school to university. The deliberations included in the book are "dispersed meditations" with an insight into innovative teaching and learning and evaluation of English.

We are still deliberating and trying to draw out an action plan for English teaching, learning and evaluation at School/College/ University level. on the lines given in draft NEP 2019 through the upcoming Bharatiya Shiksha Board aiming at alignment of national and global goals with due emphasis on character building, man making and nation building. We need to work on each aspect separately and design the course structure and the syllabi in near future. All suggestions are welcome and we plan to work with participatory approach. We hope that the papers published in the book will ignite the creativity and curiosity in the minds of the academicians involved in the process of educating the young generation.

We wish to thank the enthusiastic participants and the most renowned resource persons like Prof. Kapil Kapoor, Prof. Kavita Sharma, Dr. Elaine Boyd, Prof. C. B. Sharma, Mr. Vineet Joshi and others who gave us insights and directions to work further in the respective field.

We would like to express our gratitude to the UGC and Mrs. Neelima Sharma from Trinity College London for being instrumental in organising this International seminar. The team members from the English Department, Dr. Sucheta Chaturvedi, Ratnakar Kumar and Ojaswini Hooda deserve special mention for their assistance to this endeavour.

Pratyush Vatsala

1

Classroom 2.0: Incorporating ICT and Theatre for an Effective Learning Environment for ESL

— *Srishti Gupta*

Language acquisition in the early years stems from mimicking one's environment. A conscious study of language can be an interesting as well as a harrowing experience for students, especially when it comes to English, because of the pressure to 'improve English' a misnomer that students often use. Recently, there have been two major changes in the curriculum of Functional English at Delhi University, the introduction of a compulsory module on communicative English and application-based evaluation of language skills. This paper originates from my experience of teaching these papers in Delhi University. Some of these students were first generation English learners. To engage the diverse cohort. I used some non-traditional methods of teaching. Through this paper I attempt to show how certain activities can be easily used for first generation learners of English for enhancing the process of learning.

The main focus of my paper lies in presenting the classroom activities, improvisation exercises, Spin-A-Yarn and so on, that form an essential part of my pedagogy. These activities perform the role of bridging the gap between the traditional classrooms and the college coursework, the prerequisite for which is original thinking. They have been used during classroom sessions as well as for assessment. They also complement the changes in the curriculum in the University. They can be used as a means of continuous informal evaluation. They cover various aspects of language teaching, from grammar and reading to speaking and listening skills. I begin by sharing two activities, I have used for formal assessment. In the next section, I proceed to briefly discuss some pedagogical tools that have been used in Information and Communication Technology (ICT)-based language learning, followed by the application of Theatre in Language Learning (TiLL).

In CBSE class 12th examination, the English paper comprises 40 percent of literature-based assessment. Similarly, in the old syllabus, before the introduction of CBCS, approximately 30-40 percent of the paper component would be related to literature. The assessment of this section earlier was on the basis of answers which would reproduce the facts or a limited bank of questions that the students would prepare using guidebooks. I will discuss the phenomenon of dependence on guidebooks later in the paper. The current pattern of Core English paper for first year students of English in the University, does away with this. The papers evaluate language skills using unseen passages and poems and composition based on the same. The emphasis on Functional English is even more evident in the introduction of filing an FIR and RTI, composing tweets and Facebook passages as a part of the formal curriculum.

The following activities are based on my experience of teaching a course on "English Language through Literature", a course for students scoring 80 percent and above in their class 12th English examination. While teaching the Unit on "Reading Everyday Texts" for the same course, I followed the method of close textual analysis of the suggested readings. There were three readings on contemporary topics, farmer suicides, selfies and refugees. In the class discussions, we focused on the understanding of root words to make out the meaning of a new word and the choice of particular words in particular contexts. The end semester examination of the paper has 20 marks writing section based on the comprehension passages in the paper. Additionally, there were two internal assessments for the course, one to test reading and writing and the other to test their speaking and listening skills.

Taking a leaf out of the methodology of setting composition questions, I asked students to prepare for their Internal Assessment by reading around the topics of the prescribed readings. For their evaluation, I asked the students to write from the perspective of the afflicted in the three essays, a daughter who wishes to marry a farmer, but her parents were against the match, a woman diagnosed with selfitis, and a displaced child. Most students answered the question about farmers. The focus of the article discussed in class was on the fact that an increasing number of fathers are unwilling to marry off their daughters into households where farming was the primary source of income. I observed that a lot of the students' writing focused on elaborating the question statement and recreating the problem. Very few students explored other aspects of the given situation, for example the deeper emotional problem or the solutions to it. Even when they did, they preferred reporting the arguments rather than exploring the thought process. I observed that while writing the students want to stay in their comfort zone in the realms of the information that were already provided. By providing keywords, we circumscribe the narrative to a path unfamiliar to the student. This would in turn encourage what Malvika Rai calls "the product approach", that is, looking at writing as a perfect finished product. She argues that "the process approach to writing ... helps the writer to transform his/her experience into knowledge." (35)

In my experience, students look forward to stories. Through the other assessment, I wanted to explore creative composition which would allow space for their own thoughts. For the assessment of speaking and listening skills, I asked students to participate in a session of Spin-a-Yarn, while I observed their expression and creativity and marked them accordingly. A theme was decided by the students. They arranged their benches in a circle and each of them was to speak three statements to take the story forward. The students created a wonderful story of four girls who were at a concert, complete with exciting plot twists and change of locations, by the end of the round of 40 girls, we had visited a hospital as well as a police station, all while the protagonists completed their homework, attended tuitions only for one of them to wake up and realise it was all a dream. The story was complete with specific characteristics of the characters, recalling characters introduced earlier, creation of plot twists and resolving them within the narrative. Some students would feel stuck and were not able to think of anything impromptu. I would encourage them to focus on a specific instance or ask the previous speaker to repeat her statements and they would eventually take the story forward. When the second last student introduces a new character, I pointed out why it acts like a challenge for the last person who has to complete the story. I made sure I used positive vocabulary so as to distinguish my feedback from pointing out mistakes. The last student sealed the story neatly and then we discussed how the narrative had proceeded pooling in the ideas of the students and guiding them to build on the points I felt would help them compose better. Thus, creating narratives was a task that the students not only enjoyed, but displayed much more creativity than is reflected in their answer scripts.

These and other simple activities as elaborated on further in the paper can be easily conducted in a classroom. We are habituated to the use of ICT in our use of e-groups on WhatsApp and Facebook, in addition to Google Drive to communicate with students. Tom Rank et al. show how ICT can help language learners in smart classrooms. He exemplifies this through two activities to understand the choice and use of words can be outlined on a screen in different colours. In a poem, colouring different sound units in different colours, shows the use of alliteration in the text. In an excerpt from *Much Ado about Nothing* by Shakespeare, the words 'you, your, yours etc' are highlighted in a different colour from 'thee, thy, thou'. It is visually evident from the activity that the more formal form of address was used by elders and people in a position of power (19-21). Students become more comfortable with the use of word processing software. Rank, Warren and Millum compile a huge list of activities that have been used to facilitate better understanding of the text.

A school teacher in Birmingham, asked students to make a video game trailer on the basis of their reading of Dr. Jekyll and Mr. Hyde and watching some trailers of video games in a gothic setting (Rank 62-63). Practicing skimming through texts, which is a part of the curriculum of the 'Language through Literature' paper, I have mentioned previously, helps the students approach an unseen passage by giving them an idea of what is in store for them. If students get into the habit of using this method, it will be a useful skill in completing their paper in time. An activity suggests the use of collages of the words of a text arranged randomly, in different sizes. As a 'rapid-fire' exercise the students can try and guess what is being talked about in the text. This makes them familiar with diction and register. The activity is based on the school of Corpus Linguistics. Tools like Wordle help in the creation of these word collages (29-31). Another case study used by Rank was conducted in Australia where students of 12-13 years in age, developed a script for a video on Australia (121-2). The teacher facilitated the sub division of topics and diverse use of genres like docu-drama, interview, expert to camera and so on.

These activities are equipment intensive and such use of Information Technology for language education requires an overhaul of the curriculum and infrastructure of language education. While this model has the potential of changing the face of language pedagogy, its applicability in Indian education is debatable. Many teachers already use ICT by bringing in audio visual resources like, watching films, whether feature or animation, and other videos to supplement the instruction of a text. For providing a counter perspective to D. H. Lawrence's poem, "The

Last Lesson", I showed the music video of the song "We Don't Need No Education" by the British band Pink Floyd to the class and it led to a very fruitful discussion. Various institutions tap the potential of ICT in providing platforms for collaboration of resources, where students need not get into logistical hassles of meeting their classmates out of college for a group activity. They can collaborate remotely. However, these approaches are also dependent on the understanding that ICT is something external that we can put to use for language education. In reality, ICT is in our hands, and its presence has made a paradigm shift in our student's lived experience. This is where the use of drama comes into the picture.

With the exponential advancement in ICT, the stimuli of the student have also changed. In a research conducted by Nidhi Kunwar, she observes that the topic given to the students is very distanced from the reality of the students. As a consequence, their expression is either completely copied or at least heavily influenced from guidebooks or exemplary writing, in the students' opinion. Kunwar concludes that 'Right Writing' is encouraged in Indian classrooms. She says "rather than creating 'writers', we are creating 'copying machines' in our schools" (17). This is reflected when the students write their first college examinations and if they are unable to answer a particular question, they simply re-write the question as the answer. They believe that the answer lies in the question and not in their understanding or expression. Kunwar says that the teacher's feedback plays a crucial role in determining the students' understanding of language. If answer scripts are corrected without bothering only about spelling and grammatical errors, it may help divert a focus laid on the written product. It is only when the choice of topic as well as the diction is alien to the students, that they copy.

Thus, another challenge of ELT in the university is to introduce students to the idea of writing for oneself. To create students who compose instead of reproducing from other sources, their minds need to be reprogrammed to accept writing as a process involving thought as well as perseverance. One of the ways of achieving this is to introduce composition exercises, both oral as well as written, centred around topics which the students can relate with. Additionally, formats of writing can also be explored in tandem with a knowledge of the space where a student uses the language. Most students use Instant Messaging apps. Understanding the interest of the students facilitates the teacher in creating activities. Some classroom activities that I have used, based on my observations are as follows.

To teach dialogue writing, I divided students into groups of two and asked them to write a WhatsApp conversation with their partner. The topic I gave them was very simple. They had to enquire about their friend's plan of meeting them in the evening. I gave them plot markers like, acceptance or rejection of the invite, finalising the logistical details, plans for a meal and so on. The learners enjoyed the exercise. Their reliance on abbreviations was heavy, but they were able to create a dialogue which went beyond "Hi! How are you?". Some of them ventured into using emojis to make the conversation more realistic. As an exercise in expository writing, creating an FAQ or Frequently Asked Questions section is also an interesting activity to remove the pressure of writing about unfamiliar topics. I gave out menus in class and asked students to roleplay as a customer and a waiter and discuss about a particular dish. The customer would ask questions about a dish to the student enacting the waiter, who would respond accordingly. The ideas I suggested were enquiring about portion sizes, two specifications in terms of ingredients used or taste, and making a request for alteration. They were then asked to proceed with writing down FAQs for one dish each. In the activity, the students used the language they would use to communicate in a real-life situation. In listening to other students' questions, peer to peer learning takes place. The student observes other students' use of expression to form questions similar to theirs and tend to apply the same without knowing.

In addition to being a mode of instruction, these activities help break the ice and transmit the idea that the classroom is a safe space to bring forth their ideas without the fear of ridicule and humiliation. We underestimate the necessity and potential of ice breakers. In every class, there are usually some students whose heads are brimming with ideas, but they hesitate in speaking up. One such ice breaker that has been a useful pedagogical tool for me is conducted in groups of three. Based on the teacher's choice of the topic of instruction, it can be altered. The students are invited to come to the front of the class in groups of three. Their classmates give them a location and a situation, for example, they are playing PUBG (a multiplayer game) and they are supposed to defeat an opponent. They have to speak a phrase or a sentence, one-by-one in alphabetic order. If a students' utterance starts with M, the next student would frame a sentence starting with an N, and so on until they reach the first letter again. In these 26 sentences they have to listen to and directly respond to the person before them while trying to retain the essence of the character as well as the situation. For letters with less words, like Q, X and Z, I ask them to interpret the letters freely which lead to interesting expressions. The instructor observes their comfort, fluency and accuracy of the use of the language. Students who are not comfortable with uttering full sentences, express in words but take the narrative forward.

To focus more on vocabulary the activity can be altered in a way for the students to be allotted a fixed number of words that they can use, that is each student speaks in, say, three, five and two words respectively. The students tend to use more nouns. Activities like these help students express themselves without the fear of being judged for their language skills. If the group is odd the teacher can also participate. The students' creativity would be stimulated with the manner in which the narrative is formed. Prompts from fellow students create a friendly atmosphere and ease out the hesitation of the students in verbalising their ideas. These activities evoke the essence of traditional pedagogical tools like readers theatre. They ensure efficient learning because of the same principle as readers theatre. Learners are motivated to participate as they do not feel pinned down and that their skills are being exhibited in front of the entire classroom. In their research about the studies on Readers' Theatre, Drew and Pedersen argue that the success of Readers Theatre as a pedagogical tool for teaching of English can be attributed to the fact that it the activities are conducted in groups (4). Sean Aita also concludes in his essay on TiLL, that the use of theatre in language helps with reading and because it is a group activity. This helps greatly in overcoming the anxiety of using English publicly. Similarly, the improvisation exercises discussed above ensure participation from students because they do not feel singled out. They do not speak to their classmates, instead they speak with their classmates.

The use of conventional theatre exercises for language teaching is exemplified in an essay by Paul Davies, wherein he looks at theatrical activities like mime, role play, creating simulations and script writing as tools for ELT. Unfortunate as it may seem, today, very few students have actually watched plays being performed in a theatre. In their time spent on social media, I have observed that the interest of many students of Delhi University is captured by short vines, which depict instances from daily life. These videos posted on video hosting sites like YouTube and TikTok showcase incidents, which may be as simple as cooking or walking to the market, and explore humour, drama, archetypal characters and so on. Instead of asking students to write a play, videography can be used as an effective tool for assessment. Innovative evaluation exercises break the cycle of copying. Today, the use of smartphones is common. As an assignment, students can write and submit a short video ranging from one to three minutes. For a project, the student can curate an episode of a web-series using novel characters. The instructor can provide outlines in terms of the genre to be used, a dialogue which can be interpreted in different ways, a character name or feature, a place or location that should be represented in the plot. The instructor can discuss the script with the students and students can shoot these on a mobile phone and use simple movie editing applications to edit and add transitions.

I am yet to try this in class but am of the opinion that, if some students are unable to write well, they should be given the option of non-verbal language, that is communicating without words. The instructor can work with the students to develop the plot. Situations such as sitting in a library, hiding in a corner and so on can be used to facilitate the completion of the project. The exercise of writing subtitles can be undertaken. This would encourage the student to become confident with their expression and assess their eagerness for language learning. At a later stage during the course, the student can attempt writing subtitles for the video as an exercise in descriptive writing. Writing subtitles can also prove to be engaging activity for smaller cohort sizes. The students can be given the activity of writing subtitles for a section each of a foreign language movie or a mime like Mr. Bean's show. When the students speak them out loud in class, in a sequence, it can lead to a discussion of what could be elaborated on more and how. In such a scenario, the student can take control of their learning and creativity.

To conclude, these tools help me gain better attentiveness from the students, an engagement that is crucial to efficient language pedagogy. As instructors of language sometimes teachers have their own share of apprehensions about exploring these options as pedagogical tools. In her essay, Judith Gray Royka analyses the reasons for the apprehensions ranging from under confidence due to not being a theatre practitioner and dismissing theatre as play and not a method of education. She provides suggestions to alleviate these concerns by breaking the myths of theatrical activities being time consuming, ineffective and requiring professional expertise. Through this paper, I have managed to scrape only the tip of the iceberg. Adapting current pedagogical tools to incorporate the content that interests students on the internet and the creation of a methodology that prioritises 'process-oriented learning' over 'product-oriented learning' increases the effectivity of language learning. Based on my reading of L. Saranraj and K Meenakshi's research which elucidates how the students of English in a famous engineering college in Tamil Nadu are "extremely affected by language anxiety" (4) I have also highlighted the potential role of such activities play in facilitating the overcoming the language related anxiety of learners of English as a Second Language. As most of the activities are based on real life use of language, various transversal skills are also transferred in the process. I hope these would prove useful pedagogical tools for English Language Teaching.

Works Cited

Aita, Sean. "The Theatre in Language Learning (TiLL) Model: Exploring Theatre as Pedagogy in the L2 Environment" *Scenario,* vol. 3, no. 1, 2009, pp. 64-80.

Davies, Paul. "The Use of Drama in English Language Teaching" *TESL Canada Journal,* vol. 8, no. 1, 1990, pp. 87-99.

Drew, Ion and Roar Pederson, "Readers Theatre: A Different Approach to English for Struggling Readers". *Acta Didactica Norge,* vol. 4, no. 1, art. 7, 2010.

Kunwar, Nidhi. "Right Writing' in Classrooms: Learning to be Artificial". *Language and Language Teaching,* vol. 4, no. 1, 2015, pp. 15-19.

Loganathan, Saranraj & Meenakshi, K.. "The Influence of Anxiety in Second Language Learning: A Case Study with Reference to Engineering Students in Tamil Nadu, India." *Indian Journal of Science and Technology,* vol. 9, no. 42, 2016, (10.17485/ijst/2016/v9i42/102044).

Rai, Malvika. "Writing in Indian Schools: The Product Priority". *Language and Language Teaching,* vol 4, no. 1, 2015, pp. 32-36.

Rank, Tom, Chris Warren and Trevor Millum. *Teaching English Using ICT.* A&C Black, 2011.

Royka, J. "Overcoming the Fear of Using Drama in English Language Teaching". *The Internet TESL Journal,* vol. 8, no. 6, 2002. Available at: http://iteslj.org/Articles/Royka-Drama.html. Accessed 20 January 2020.

2

Teaching Spoken English to Grade 5 through Co-operative Learning using Formulaic Sequences

— *Harpreet Kaur*

The Jumpstart Pilot Project was an action research project since the main aims were to observe, describe, analyze, and interpret the facts and characteristics affecting the language learning process of students. It was an attempt to determine the effectiveness of learning process that used formulaic sequences through bilingual whole language cooperative learning and social media (whatsapp) in teaching Basic Spoken English to Grade 5 students, with first generation learners in majority. Participants were 41 Grade 5 students in a government school in Delhi.

Introduction

Need of Spoken English

School education needs to prepare students for 21st century skills for leading a productive life as a complex, energetic, tech savvy individual in a globalised working environment. Good English Speaking skills provide a significant advantage to the individual as it is a skill favoured by employers. Being a well groomed communicator in English provides greater chances of employment as many companies have an international presence and even as entrepreneurs or freelancers working in a liberalised globalised economy as India, both socially and businesswise, speaking in English is gainful and almost a basic competency.

In the face of this imperative of present times, sadly, we still have a majority of students lacking English spoken skills in schools across the government and private sector especially in the primary grades in India, even in the metro cities, especially Delhi. The situation is that even students who can read and write well in English have great hesitation in speaking in English. The need of the hour: a well-rounded self-expression in Spoken English is a thing of luxury. The hesitation to speak in English continues even till XII.

Existent scenario: Imparting Spoken English Skills in Primary

Ur (1996) considered speaking as the most important skill among four skills (listening, speaking, reading, and writing) because people who know a language are referred to as speakers of that language.

So although speaking skill is the envisioned target outcome of teaching English language by eminent stakeholders of education: the curriculum setters, school managements, parents, teachers but it is not directly and adequately addressed by the curriculum, classroom teaching and the social general awareness of language learning.

Perhaps the main reason is a misconception expressed by Chaney, 1998

In the past, oral communication instruction was neglected because of the misconception that oral communication competence develops naturally over time and that the cognitive skills involved in writing automatically transfer to analogous oral communication skills.

Writing tests being the predominant testing instrument of outcome of English teaching only underscores the prevalence and depth to which this misconception is embedded. The parents and teachers hold the view that scoring well in writing tests will automatically lead the spoken skill. Thus, technically, spoken language skill is relegated to being very much as the last and the least of the adequately addressed LSRW.

The classroom teaching of spoken skill has huge stumbling blocks to negotiate like syllabus completion syndrome, shortage of teachers with spoken English proficiency, usage of traditional lecture teaching methodology, teaching language through grammar and a lack of awareness of the fact that spoken and written English are technically different from each other.

The difference in the formality of the two, the spoken and the written; influences the vocabulary, sentence length and usage of fillers to hold conversations. Plus speaking has the listening and pronunciation skill input, imperatives to be taken care of. Spoken skill requires responses of thinking and listening in dynamic, interpersonal interactions. It involves real communication with real people in everyday real life activities. To attain conversational fluency, a learner needs massive and consistent practice, the time for which is not factored enough into the curriculum, time table or classroom teaching.

Traditional teaching lecture method affords merely a passive and receptive role on the part of the students during the lessons. Furthermore, the lessons are stories or poems wherein the foremost and paramount focus is testing the text for information followed by teaching grammar rules and structured explanations. Although, National Curriculum Framework discourages this approach, to many teachers this is the approach by which they studied in their schools and this is the approach by which they explain in class too. The parent community (especially parents of first generation learners) too till date equate grammar with language proficiency and are of the view that knowing grammar rules by the book, being able to do grammar exercises and some vocabulary, automatically leads to good speaking skills.

Concepts involved

Teaching Speaking

The main goal of teaching speaking is communicative efficiency. Teaching speaking means helping learners develop their ability to interact successfully in the target language. To do so, one must have communicative competence.

- Dr. Ahmed Maher Mahmoud Al Nakhalah, Al Quds Open University-Palestine /Gaza

Richards, Platt, and Weber (as cited in Nunan, 1999) defined the characteristics of communicative competence as: Thus, to help students enhance their speaking skills, the teacher must help students improve their grammar, enrich their vocabulary, and manage interactions in terms of who says what, to whom, when, and about what.

Cooperative Learning

Cooperative Learning is a teaching arrangement that refers to small, heterogeneous groups of students working together to achieve a common goal (Kagan, 1994). Students work together to learn and are responsible for their teammates' learning as well as their own. The basic elements are:

1. Positive Interdependence
2. Individual Accountability
3. Equal Participation
4. Simultaneous Interaction

Hundreds of studies have been undertaken to measure the success of cooperative learning as an instructional method regarding social skills, student learning, and achievement across all levels from primary grades through college. The general consensus is that cooperative learning can and usually does result in positive student outcomes in all domains (Johnson & Johnson, 1999).

Why Cooperative Learning for Spoken English?

1. Productive Language Skills: Spoken and Written skills are better acquired through peer interaction rather than taught-down-by-teacher. Peer learning and group dynamics provide a ready-at-hand-set-up for real-time application and interplay of interpersonal language skills. i.e. real-time communication development.

2. Group Learning provides the requisite set up. Peer learning encourages even the weakest student to ask questions. In a traditional lecture teaching set up the weak students never muster up the courage to ask questions. Encouraging a student to ask questions is the best way to get the student to start with communication skills.

3. When the students try to understand and achieve learning outcomes of the English lesson among themselves, they communicate, differ in opinion, explain, clarify and negotiate the meaning of the syllabus lesson among themselves. Thus the process there is acquisition of life skills along with the subject matter. Positive group and individual behaviour dynamics set into the language acquisition process. The students learn from and teach each other. People learn the most by teaching – Peter Drucker.

4. The group dynamics in Cooperative Learning promotes development of leadership skills. Interpersonal skills are activated besides language learning. The brighter students assume the role of teachers and guides. Students weaker at language skills feel more comfortable asking questions and seeking explanations amongst their peers. Interpersonal communication for asking and telling meanings, negotiating the meaning of text as a team happens in real-time. All students learn to finish a task together. A requisite peer hand holding for both comprehending the text and then thinking up language to answer is set into motion. The cooperative learning set up affords the learner to see that there are many students in class who have the same problems in language learning. The learner does not feel alone as a seeker of knowledge. Every member of team feels valued for contributing something or the other for performance of the team. The weaker students

learn to work around the comprehension and language synthesising issues.

Why Bilingual approach for imparting spoken skills in English?

Bilingual often refers to an individual or group of individuals who routinely uses two different languages.

For this project, it was important to think about how teachers, parents and the school itself, cooperate with the process of language learning outside the classroom. Once students leave the English class, the language they hear in the schools, homes, and public places is their mother tongue. Bilingual approach is proposed especially to engage the stake of the first generation parents in the language acquisition process.

Bilingual approach is proposed to constructively serve comprehension of L2. The aim is that the students pick up L2 with full comprehension and the formulaic sequences used should not be learnt by rote. It is foreseen that the bright students who know the meaning of L2 sequences will be taking up the role of peer teachers within groups. Students will be required to collect information from their immediate peers, family and neighbourhood as is the case in real life. Purely L2 approach will not serve this purpose.

Jonassen (1999) states that: "Meaningful learning' requires knowledge to be constructed by the learner, not transmitted from the teacher to the student".

Bilingual approach will be required to create language contexts in and out of the classroom, increasing in this way, the students' learning opportunities, due to the fact that learning is an active process in which students construct ideas about language by engaging themselves in it (Dewey, 1938).

Care will be taken that positive cross language facilitation remains at play and negative (MT Interference) is minismised and used constructively to identify, discourage and create awareness amongst the participants.

Use of Formulaic Sequences and why?

Formulaic sequences (FS) are frequently used by native speakers and have been found to help non-native speakers gain fluency too. It was hypothesized that explicitly teaching FS to classroom ESL learners would increase the use of such language, which could further result in increased second language (L2) fluency within the targeted 14 days.

Most of the FS used will be task based sentence beginnings along with functional vocabulary.

The participants will read, hear, understand FS English and practice speaking using a task-based approach.

Use of Whatsapp Messenger in spoken skills teaching learning and why?

Social network refers to networked tools that allow people to meet, interact and share ideas, artifacts and interests with each other (Anderson, 2010). This social network has opened up new opportunities of interaction and collaboration between teachers and learners.

The use of social network has become popular in everyday communication. It is even used for collaborative learning especially in language learning.

The most recent popular social network nowadays is WhatsApp application. WhatsApp Messenger is a proprietary, crossplatform instant messaging application for smart phones. In addition to text messaging, users can send each other images, video, and audio media messages (Wikipedia, 2013). WhatsApp allows its users to use their Internet connection to send messages to each other. WhatsApp is like a chat program for mobile phones. Smart phones are becoming increasingly popular and WhatsApp is available for almost all Smartphone.

Use of Whatsapp Messenger was proposed for the following reasons:

1. The learners would not feel that acquiring Spoken skill was anything to study. It would be seen as fun.

2. Since the owner of the mobile phone would be a parent, the parent would by default become a secondary participant to the process as a monitoring agent and a videographer too. It is expected that since the students would be recording videos of spoken English tasks at home, they would be discussing or working out the language and nitty-gritty with their parent. Thus, the parent would become the first spectator of the child's performance. A parent-child collaborative learning partnership is anticipated to get fostered through the program. Language acquisition will be extended and continued from within the classroom to homes too.
3. It is anticipated that both learners and parents would proudly love to share the 'English speaking videos' with friends, neighbours etc and sharing these would increase the fun and the motivation levels for learners exponentially.
4. The video sharing on whatsapp will help the learners gain self-assessment insights and thus will put them on a path of self-improvement and learning for life.
5. It will create an opportunity for appointing Language Monitors and such other leadership roles from amongst the learners. Whatsapp Messenger is seen as the most vital component of the program required to put an ecosystem of learning with all the three stakeholders teacher, parent and student actively taking part in the process.

Setting up the Pilot

Initiation: In agreement with the Principal & Head Mistress the action research project was started. It was agreed that a batch of students will be trained to overcome their hesitation to speak in English in 14 days.

In the talks for administering Jumpstart Program in the school to the students, The Principal deemed it fit that the program be given full flexibility and that HM and team will assist it.

Pilot Batch Logistics

Grade 5 was chosen as it is placed strategically as the transition grade between primary and middle school. Additionally, this is the grade wherein many learners would have managed to gain reading skills required to read the text used in the program.

41 Grade 5 students were selected by class teachers. The batch composition was 10 students from each of the 4 sections of Grade 5 in the school. Amongst each of the 10 students per section chosen, 6 students were linguistically and academically challenged, 2 students were average performers and 2 were above average performers. At least 2 students per class had weighty issues like low attendance and work completion across subjects. The time of the school selected was the assembly time so that studies in any other periods in the time table were not affected. It was one hour everyday. Due to academic priorities, holidays and other school engagements the 14 days were not continuous at a stretch. It was approximately three days in a week that could be afforded.

Baseline Tests

Baseline tests were conducted in the classroom (the Resource room of the school) itself. The tests were not more than 3 – 4 minutes of duration. The tests were designed to gauge the basic functional vocabulary, sentence construction and the extent of speaking-in-English-hesitation that the learners had at the beginning of the program. 2 students were called at a time and were given 3 speaking tasks in the following sequence:

1. Introduce yourself.
2. Describe a picture
3. Talk to each other on a topic (topics of interest, immediate environment and real life activities such as friends, family, birthday parties, holidays, ice creams, junk food, fruits, naughty things children do, when do parents not like etc.

Video recordings of the tests were made on mobiles

It took 3 days to conduct the test for the batch.

Midline Tests

Two speaking tasks of the Baseline Test were also used for midline performance video recordings. These video recordings were done by the students themselves and shared on the group. So the midline was entirely informal, learner conducted and at learner's home, mostly with participation of parents.

Endline Tests

A public event with parents and teachers as audience was conceived as endline test. This was done keeping in line with the main goal of the project and i.e. to remove the hesitation of the students to speak in English for representing themselves in public.

Classroom Proceedings: 14 days of Pilot

Groups were made in the class. Each section was a group. Participants were provided with booklets with formulaic sequences. The first module was about making introductions of self, friends, family and any other person.

Elicitation technique was used to impart thinking skills for the topic. The students were first asked about what things they would want to know about any person. After the brainstorming they looked up the booklets for working out the language. Students who could understand the text helped the students who couldn't. Everyone wrote their introductions in the booklet and practised speaking and pronunciation in pairs.

There were a lot of issues encountered in terms of setting the pace of language learning in the class. It was found that students weak in academics are generally not in a habit of paying attention in the class. They lacked the cognizance that they were present in the class to complete a certain task. Mental processes and attention span for task completion was a challenge for them. To put these on track peer leaders were appointed in each group.

Diaries were also provided to children to keep noting any new words and sentences or a group of words they would like to speak for presenting their thoughts.

A scoring system for teams was put up on the charts

It was noted by the Head Mistress that some students who had good comprehension levels in English but were never found to speak in English in school before, started talking to teachers in English. They started asking questions and for directions in English. This happened on the first day itself.

On the first day itself, the students were found jotting down language into their diaries. In about two-three days, it was shared by one of the teachers that the Jumpstart students were seen to be engaged with Jumpstart booklets in regular class time such as free periods etc. The students showed interest in practising from the booklets in school itself.

On the 6th day a Whatsapp group Jumpstart Spoken English Program was started. As per instructions from the Principal, the HM to put up a message to parents that "If any parent had concerns regarding whatsapp usage regulation, they should contact the Principal". The students were to upload the spoken tasks onto the group. And they were o be given points and feedback as per their performance.

Over 240 videos were uploaded by students in a period of 13 days. The videos were of introducing oneself, a friend and parents. Brainstorming and group discussions were held on what would be the right things to ask or talk about the individual to be introduced. And what language was to be used. The booklets were used like starters for language learning. It was found that many students improvised and added many things to their booklets and spoken tasks.

Also started off were *'How to say it in English;* charts in classrooms and at homes too. This was a strategic deliberation to extend the language learning out of the Jumpstart Classroom into school time, into the peer group, family and neighbourhood. Students were supposed to write sentences of Hindi of which they wanted to know the English translation. And any student or teacher could write the translations. English teacher was supposed to keep an eye on the language corrections required. Points were allotted per sentence per word written. One section started off the very first day in great enthusiasm. Two sections responded the third or fourth day. And the fourth section had some chart-putting-up delay. 10 children made How to say it in English charts at home and parents were very happy. Photos of these charts were shared on the group. Separate marks for home charts were allotted.

During the session of discussion on how to introduce parents, it was found that many students did not know their parents' qualifications, company name, work profile and designation. The students then understood the requirement of the same and decided that they needed to ask questions. One of the students' happened to make a Question Answer video of introducing the parent. And many other students too followed suit. Every student improved.

In order to minister leadership qualities, Diary Monitors, Grammar Monitors, Work Completion Monitors, Writing Marks Monitors were appointed.

Students with better language skills were asked to help give feedback on videos shared in the group. Every video was allotted marks according to vocabulary used, pronunciation and sentence construction. Vocabulary, pronunciation, grammar corrections and body language tips were given. Many students made improved second videos. Some parents too gave encouraging likes and remarks.

Attempts were made to keep the audience on the group engaged. Once, when it was announced that a task for a big score was to be announced, parents were found to be very keen on getting the information and getting it done by their child.

Participation by some of the most academically challenged students in the group too was low. A part of the obstacle lay at the parents' end too.

On the 12th day the program agenda was finalised in discussion with students. The students were facilitated to decide what was to be included and in what sequence. They were told that the program had to be designed in such a way that the parents should come to know about everything that was being done for the language learning. Hesitant students who had never spoken on stage or in public were given anchoring roles. Each and every student had to go on stage and speak in English. Video recordings would be made of the each and every students' presentation.

Day 13 went off in rehearsing for the event.

Day 14 the Endline Readings Day. Parents Workshop cum Student Presentation Event day was held in the school senior library. First off a parent workshop was held wherein the parents were educated about ways by which Spoken English is gained with great difficulty. A myths vs. reality scenario was presented on the same. Different stages of language development were discussed so that the parents could handle and participate in the language learning process with their child, more constructively.

Student Diaries and class How to say it in English charts were also displayed at the venue. After the Parents workshop and student presentations, a parent feedback session was held.

Results

Post Day 14, a survey was done with the parents the results of which were as follows:

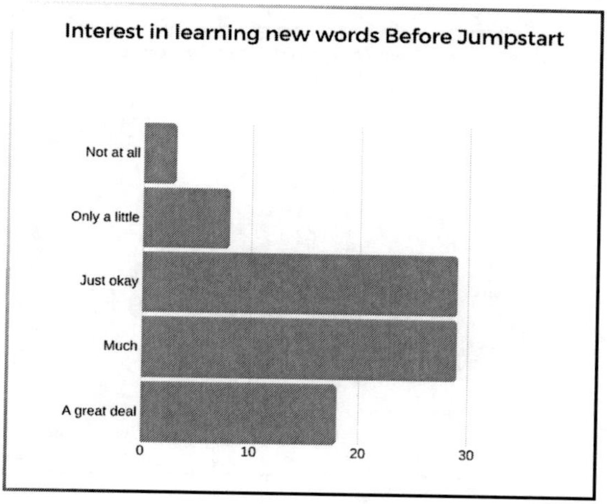

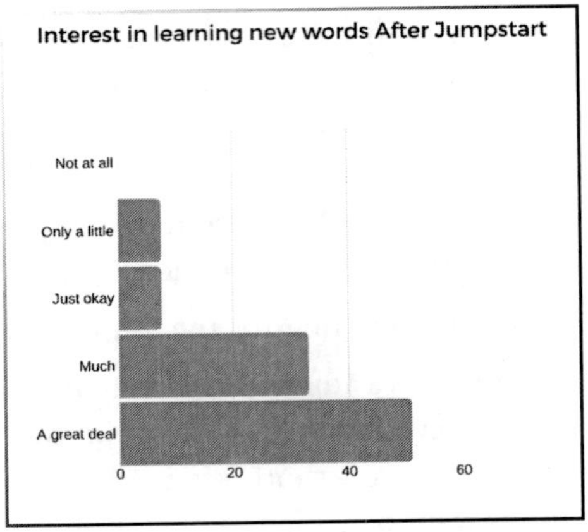
Interest in learning new words After Jumpstart
Not at all
Only a little
Just okay
Much
A great deal
0
20
40
60

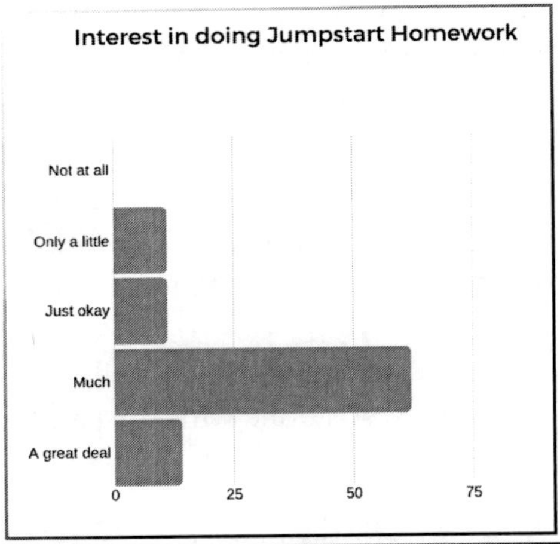
Interest in doing Jumpstart Homework
Not at all
Only a little
Just okay
Much
A great deal
0
25
50
75

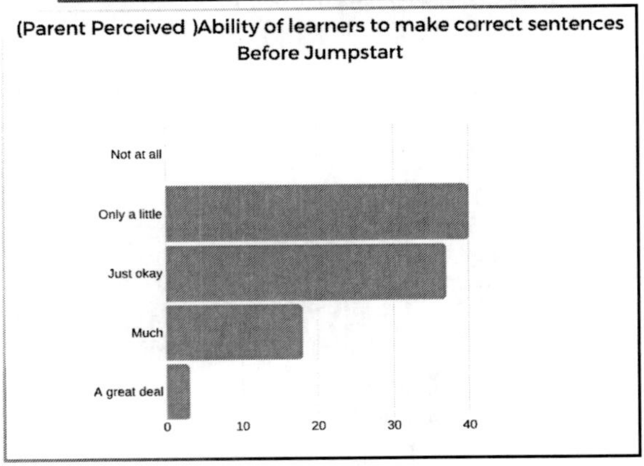
(Parent Perceived)Ability of learners to make correct sentences Before Jumpstart
Not at all
Only a little
Just okay
Much
A great deal
0
10
20
30
40

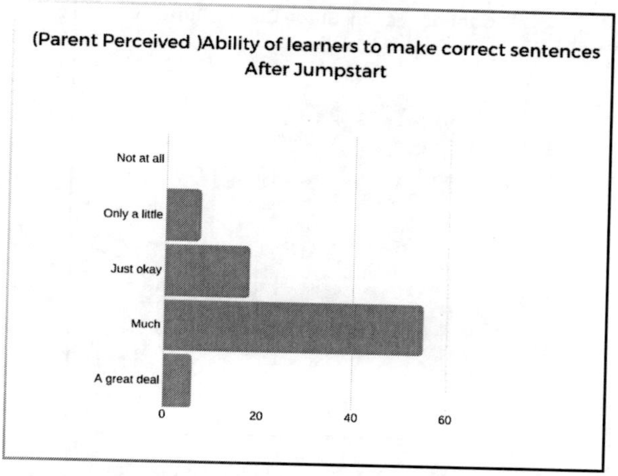
(Parent Perceived)Ability of learners to make correct sentences After Jumpstart
Not at all
Only a little
Just okay
Much
A great deal
0
20
40
60

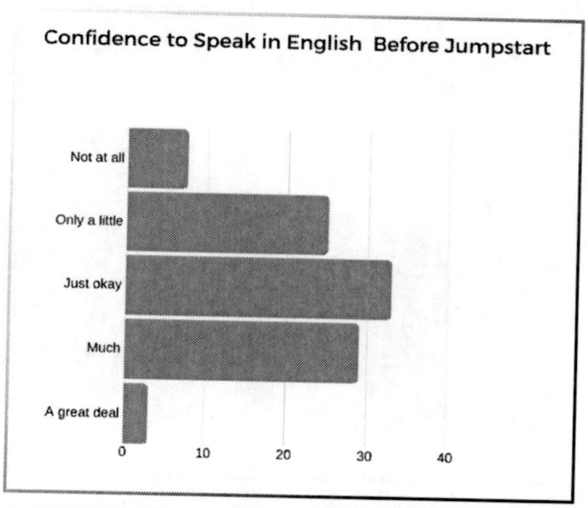
Confidence to Speak in English Before Jumpstart
Not at all
Only a little
Just okay
Much
A great deal
0
10
20
30
40

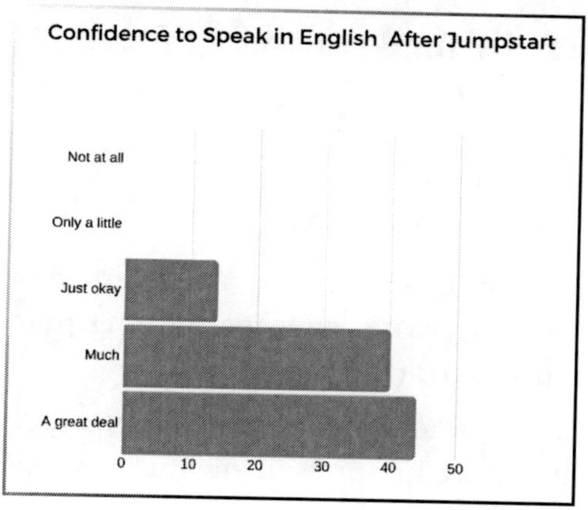
Confidence to Speak in English After Jumpstart
Not at all
Only a little
Just okay
Much
A great deal
0
10
20
30
40
50

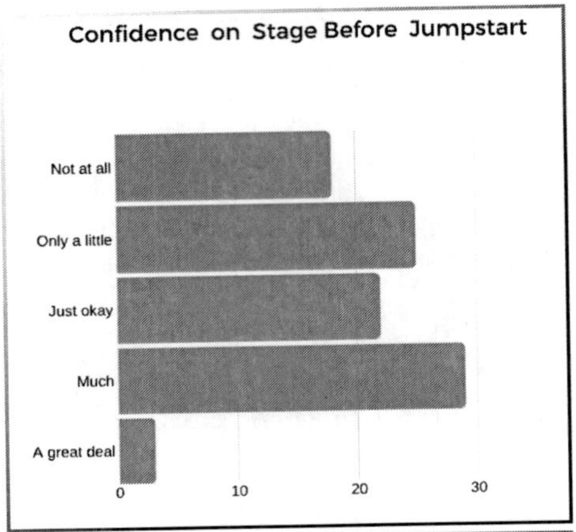

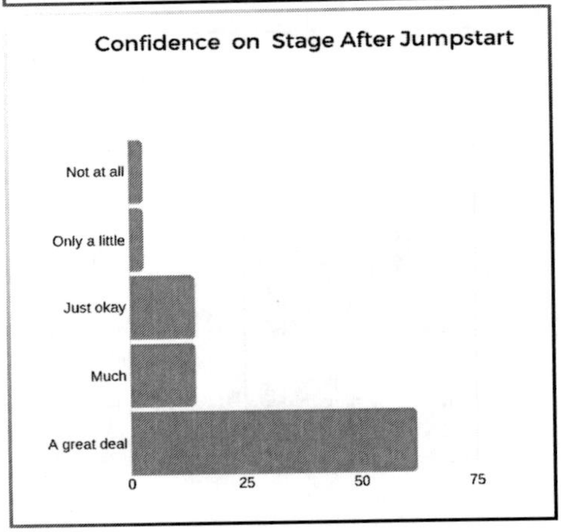

Feedback by the Principal & Head Mistress: (sent by whatsapp)

Other Observations

Participant Behaviour Observations

Positive attitude towards acquiring skills, academic orientation, team work, familiarity with language learning process were seen building up in participants.

1. The most academically and linguistically challenged students showed improvement in classroom response and

task completion along with now attempting to comprehend the text (as reported by an English teacher of students), which they never used to do before. Even the most tongue tied in class student now spoke in the team and attempted to answer in the class. They felt great at having spoken on stage in English. It was a big achievement for them and their parents.

2. Students having academic smarts showed interest in making team members perform. They told about the behavioural issues they were facing and asked for leadership tips. They acknowledged that their stage confidence had improved immensely. Their vocabulary and sentence making had become much better.
3. Although Grammar Monitors were appointed amongst the students but their contribution could not be streamlined. Their functioning can be better structured and integrated into the team work.

Parent Trends

1. Parents of academically bright students were generally the first movers in the Whatsapp group. They took great initiative in uploading the videos.
2. Parents of academically challenged students were slow to respond. These parents had lesser interest in the child's project engagement. But once they picked up, there was no looking back.

Non-Jumpstart Students of Grade 5 Response

Jumpstart got recognised as a Student Smartening Up program. In the words of the HeadMistress, Jumpstart students acquired a sort of a special status in the school. At least 10 students of Grade 5 requested to join the program. Permission was granted to them.

Conclusion

Use of formulaic sequences with bilingual whole language approach administered through cooperative learning to Grade 5 was successful in building up Spoken English skills in Grade 5 students, even the academically and linguistically challenged students. Use of Whatsapp Messenger most remarkably contributed to the success of the pilot. It strategically implicitly and unhesitatingly roped in the parents into the language learning process as active observers, monitors and guides.

The pilot built up a healthy parents and student community driven for the purpose. A healthy competition was set in with marks allotment for not only the spoken tasks but all small and big tasks of responsibility taking.

The goal of familiarising students and parents with the process of working out language was achieved. The hesitation of students for speaking in English was overcome to a great extent.

Ripple effects of the program were noticed in the immediate neighbourhood, family, cousins and friends of students.

A factor that contributed to the success of the pilot was that it did not disturb the school time table or other subject classes of the students.

Recommendations

Jumpstart Program is recommended for Grade 5 with first generation learners in mixed ability groups. An afterthought is that it can also be run for Grade 4 and Grade 6.

It can be easily implemented in government and low budget schools requiring only the following infrastructural provisions: within existing classroom, course booklets, chalk, duster, writing board, charts, notice boards and mobiles.

A course of a 100 days i.e. a 100 hours in an academic year is recommended for a consolidated transformation in the Spoken English Proficiency and personality development of the students along with Leadership skills.

Video recordings took quite a space in the mobile. Hence making available a basic video recording mobile with a decent memory is recommended. Otherwise Facebook as a community platform can be tried which will help mitigate the mobile memory space clogging issue.

Since the course content is basic, any shortcomings in the teacher English language competence can also be fixed up within about a week – ten days training. Teachers will need to be trained in cooperative learning which can be managed in 2 – 3 days.

It is recommended that a post program, survey of the academic performance of all the students should be done to gauge the ripple effect of the program on overall academic results.

3

How to Collocate Words

— ***Dr. Yashu Rai***

"Why bother with the right word; people understand me well enough" is the typical response of the uncaring speaker to any criticism of his usage – that is of the way he talks or writes. But do people understand such a speaker even if they understand him; what is their impression of him? Using the right word at right time is rather like wearing appropriate clothing for the occasion; It is a courtesy to others and a favour to yourself – a method of presenting yourself well in the eyes of the world. Just as dressing appropriately can help one to feel more confident and to act more effectively; so speaking and writing appropriately can help one to reach clearer decisions and persuade others to agree with you. Sloppy language makes for muddled thinking.

All of us use words in each act of verbal or written communication during a long span of rigorous academic work and even after that. And many of us use words without knowing their exact meaning often. That can prove to be dangerous. A good command over English and word meanings is essential to achieve clarity in language. In fact, this becomes all the more essential when we realise that words are similar but they are absolutely appear to be similar to others in their meaning. And we start making guesses that can get us into trouble.

As English is the second language for us i.e. Indians. It is lethal to operate with assumption while using the language. For what we intend to say might be completely different from what we intend up saying just because we do not check the dictionary when we learn a language. We did not learn how individual words combine together in phrases and sentences.

Does the following sentence sound right? Meals will be served outside on the terrace, weather *allowing*.

It seems to be an acceptable English sentence and the meaning is not very difficult to understand.

They will give us meals outside if the weather is good enough.

However, it will sound odd to native English speaker. Because the common combination is, in fact, not *weather allowing* but weather *permitting*.

This is something that a native speaker knows but which we have to learn. It does not help that allow and permit have similar meanings. But only *permit* is right in this context.

The way in which words belong together as weather and permitting do is known as *Collocation*.

We can talk about both:

Thick fog and dense fog

Thick smoke and dense smoke

Thick forest and dense forest

The meaning is the same. We cannot talk about a person having dense hair (incorrect). The combination does not sound right even though it world easily be understood.

Dense does not collocate with hair.

We can only say *Thick hair*.

See if you can link the pairs that collocate strongly with each other

Vitally Successful

Acutely	popular
Heartily	serious
Deadly	important
Supremely	aware
Highly	sick
Immensely	confident

The answers to the linking pairs are

Vitally	important
Acutely	aware
Heartily	sick
Deadly	serious
Supremely	confident
Highly	successful
Immensely	popular

In order to write and speak natural and correct English, we must know which adjectives are used with certain nouns.

How Forcible are Right Words:

Your talk, like almost anyone else's is often a flow of words that expresses general reactions and feelings. Tones, gestures and repetitions help you to be clear and understood. But in writing your words are alone. Unless your reader guesses another meaning from the context, your words mean what they say. Get your ideas clear and then choose words to reflect them exactly. Make your sentences make sense.

It is often found that a majority of us have extremely limited awareness of how to collocate words. This not only handicaps our effort to read, write or speak but also greatly discourages learning. In this paper, a comprehensive attempt has been made to learn the meanings of many useful words which are commonly confused by a majority of us; to include as many pairs of words which pose difficulty to us.

1. You must have heard many people saying:

   I am a regular *customer* in this beauty parlour here use of customer is incorrect. They must say ; I am a regular *client* in this beauty parlour. Because when we buy something, we are customers and when we avail somebody's services; we are clients.

   It will be correct to say:

   Shopkeepers give gifts to their regular *customers*.

2. My friend gave me a *gift* on my birthday (incorrect)

   My friend gave me a *present* on my birthday (correct)

   Gift is given from superiors to inferiors;

   From rich to poor and present is given to equals.

   The rich man gave a gift of Rs. 10000/- to the poor man.

3. Rajiv Gandhi was *murdered* at Sri Perembudur, (incorrect)

   Rajiv Gandhi was *assassinated* at Sri Perembudur (correct)

   Murder is unlawful killing of any human being.

   Assassination is killing of somebody important person for money or for political motive.

4. *Moral* of our cricket team is very high these days (incorrect)

   Morale of our cricket team is very high these days (correct)

   Because moral is that which a story, event or experience teaches us. For example

   Moral of the story 'King Bruce and Spider' is 'Try' Try again.'

   Moral is a state of discipline or spirit.

5. The mother *interfered* when she saw her children quarrelling (incorrect)

   The mother *intervened* when she saw her children quarrelling (correct)

   Because *intervene* is to come in between others especially when we take action in a situation to help someone.

   Interfere is to meddle with somebody's affairs. For example:

They did not interfere with us; we did not interfere with them.

6. Jawahar Lal Nehru was very *famous* among children. Here use of *famous* is incorrect.

   Jawahar Lal Nehru was very *popular* among children.

   Because famous is known by others and popular is liked by others.

   For Example:

   MF Hussain has become famous overnight because of painting of Madhuri Dixit.

7. Living in a big city makes me feel *alone* (incorrect)

   Living in a big city makes me feel *lonely* (correct)

   Because alone means without any companion

   Lonely means sad because one has no friends

   She is feeling very *lonely* after her husband's death.

   One sentence with Lonely and Alone both:

   She lives *alone* but never feels *lonely*

8. He has a feminine voice (incorrect)

   He has an effeminate voice (correct)

   Because feminine means qualities that are supposed to be typical of women e.g.

   She looked delicately feminine in that dress.

   Effeminate is used for men having characteristics typical of women. It is a derogatory term.

9. Sachin's electrifying performance led the team glorious *triumph* (incorrect)

   Here the word should be *victory*

   Because victory means to win and triumph is the feeling of happiness that comes after victory. As: the Indian cricket team returned home in *triumph* after winning Coca-Cola Cup in Sharjah

10. He beat his son severely and was full of *penance* (incorrect)
    The correct work is "Repentance" Because Repentance is to feel sorrow about something that one had done or failed to do
    Penance is a punishment that one gives to himself to show that one is sorry for having done wrong.
    He cooked the dinner as a *penance* for forgetting his wife's birthday.
11. My little sister is afraid of cockroaches she is *coward* (incorrect)
    My little sister is afraid of cockroaches, she is a *timid* (correct)
    Because timid means easily frightened
    Coward is a person who lacks courage when facing a dangerous situation and tries to avoid it.
    People who cannot face the problems in life and commit suicide are *cowards*.
12. He *jumped* into the water to save a *sinking* child (incorrect)
    He *dived* into the water to save a *drowning* child (correct)
    Jumping into water is *diving*. Ship Sinks and person drowns. Boat capsizes.
13. Many of us do not know the difference between woman and lady.
    Now-a-days, *ladies* have become aware of their rights (incorrect)
    Now-a-day, women have become aware of their rights (correct)
    Because woman is female human being and lady is a woman of good family and social *position*.
    The lady at the tourist office told that it opens at 1 p.m.
14. The young couple *absconded* because their parents would not let them marry (incorrect)
    The young couple *eloped* because their parents would not let them marry (correct)

Abscond means to run away suddenly and secretly to avoid arrest.

Elope means to run away suddenly and secretly *to marry*.

Let's have a look at sentence with abscond.

On his way to court, he absconded from police (custody)

15. She is *bold* enough not to obey her boss (incorrect)

    She is daredevil enough not to obey her boss because daredevil is a person on who is foolishly bold and seems not to care about danger. It is derogatory.

    Bold means confident and brave. It is used in positive sense. For example

    I am not bold enough to live alone.

16. It is the *work* of the scientist to prove the propounded theories (incorrect)

    It is the job of the scientist to prove the propound theories (correct)

    Because *job* is a particular work assigned to the person.

    Work is more general.

    Everybody should work hard.

17. Children who lack the safety of parental care have disbalanced personality (incorrect)

    Children who lack the *security* of parental care have disbalanced personality (correct)

    Because security is freedom from anxiety

    Safety is freedom from danger.

    For example:

    We must observe *safety* rules

18. The little girl was *embracing* her doll (incorrect)

    The little girl was *hugging* her doll (correct)

    Because *embrace* is to hold a person in one's arms as a sign of affection. *Hug* is to put one's arms round somebody/something to show affection.

She embraced her son before leaving.

He hugged the book to his chest.

19. He is fond of *journeying* (incorrect)

He is fond of *travelling* (correct)

Because journey is particular or specific one

Travelling is used in wider sense

Series of journeys – travel

Example:

Did you have a comfortable *journey*

He plans to write a book about his *travels*

My friend is working in my place on a *momentary* basis (incorrect)

20. My friend is working in my place on a *temporary* basis

Because *momentary* means lasting for a moment only

Temporary means lasting for a *short* time

For example:

There was a *momentary* interruption during the film show.

He thought momentarily before replying

He found it difficult to *sympathize* with the working mother of two little children (incorrect)

21. He found it difficult to *empathize* with the working mother of two little children.

Because *sympathy* is the feeling of pity and sorrow for somebody

Empathy is the ability to imagine and share the feelings of other persons.

For Example:

He deserves sympathy for the way he has been treated

There is natural love and empathy between the two.

22. The police arrested that fowl *thief* and sent him to prison. (incorrect)

The police arrested that fowl *filcher* and sent him to prison

Because *thief* is a person who steals something of value
Filcher is a person who steals something of little value
e.g. Jewel Thief

23. The policeman was *following* a robber. (incorrect)
    The policeman was *pursuing* a robber
    Because *pursue* means to go after in order to capture or kill
    Follow means to come after as Monday follows Sunday
    You go first, I will follow you.
24. Their marriage has been *happy* one
    Because *happy* is a feeling of pleasure satisfaction and contentment
25. The magistrate will *give* the judgement today (incorrect)
    The magistrate will *pass* the judgement today (correct)
    Because judgement is always passed verdict is given by the jury
26. I am a regular customer of *The Tribune*
    I am a regular subscriber of *The Tribune*
    Subscriber is a person who obtains a subscription for a magazine or newspaper
27. Our English teacher is 30, she is still a *bachelor* (incorrect)
    Our English teacher is 30,
    She is still a *spinster* (correct)
    Spinster is the feminine gender of bachelor; esp. an older woman. Many are not familiar with this word.
28. We were given only 2 hrs. to attempt such a *long* paper (incorrect)
    We are given only 2 hours to attempt such a *lengthy* paper (correct)
    Because *long* is measuring from end to end. It is used for physical sense.
    Lengthy is adjective of speech &
    It is a *long* lane that has not turning
    The priest gave a lengthy discourse on morality.

29. Phoolan Devi was a *famous* dacoit (incorrect)

    Phoolan Devi was a *notorious* dacoit (correct)

    Because *famous* is well-known for good deals

    Notorious is well known for bad deed.

    It will be right to say:

    Mr. H.C. Popli is a *famous* doctor you must have heard many students saying:

30. I *read* in campus school (incorrect)

    I *study* in campus school (correct)

    Because *study* means devotion of knowledge.

    Read is to look at, understand or

    To go through printed words silently or aloud to others.

    The boy can neither read nor write.

    Can you read the time?

    For Example:

    A news reader *reads* the news.

    She does not *study* it.

    For Example:

    An author must not be too *sensitive* to criticism

    It was sensible of you to lock the door

    Sensible refers to intellect

    Sensitive refers to emotions

    For Example:

    He is being treated for typhoid

    He has been fully cured of typhoid

31. He is a very strict teacher & always does *hard* marking (incorrect)

    He is a very strict teacher & always does *strict* marking (correct)

    Because

32. Satisfaction/contentment

Satisfaction means the state of being pleased or satisfied

Contentment means not wanting more.

She gets *contentment* with very little

Your success will be a great *satisfaction* to your parents.

33. Look at these sentences:

I am *hoping for* a phone call from him.

I am *expecting* a phone call from him.

Expect is a kind of thinking. It is not an emotion. It is connected with logic.

If one expect, he has a good reason to think that is will happen.

Hope is more emotional. If one hopes for something, one wants it to happen.

I hope she writes to one soon.

I am expecting his arrival any moment.

34. The lamp was hanging from the roof (incorrect)

The lamp was hanging from the *ceiling*.

Roof is the top outer covering of building, but, car etc.

Ceiling is the top inner surface of a room, bus, car etc.

35. He was greatly *praised* for his achievements. (incorrect)

He was greatly *admired* for his achievement (correct)

Because we admire a man for what he does.

For Example:

Our guests *praised* the meal as the best they had had for years

Do not forget to *admire* the baby

36. I saw a fish *floating* in the water (incorrect)

I saw a fish *swimming* in the water (correct)

Because lifeless things *float* and living things *swim*

I saw a beat *floating* in the water is correct.

37. My brother works in sugar *factory* (incorrect)

    My brother works in sugar *mill* (correct)

    Because both factory & mill are industrial buildings but they involve different processes and produce different kinds of things. In factory, products are made and put together.

    Shoe factory, toy factory

    Mill is a building where certain raw materials are processed

    Cotton mill, paper mill

4

Empowered Learning of English Language: A Pragmatic Deconstruction

— *Garima Bhayana*

Learning as a verb literally must mean experiencing. Similarly, teaching as a verb must mean providing pedestal to experience. However, not completely does the mostly prevalent teaching method comply with the previous propositions. Teachers and Professors are rightly considered to be the guiding lights for a learner to tread the path of glorious education. The conventional techniques of board and chalk teaching, standing before a class of forty were successful until students didn't have options to explore outside the school. Now, a parallel world runs outside the classrooms, the virtual world of abundant knowledge and opportunities, communication and challenges, transference and cyber diaspora. It has led to an unlimited expansion in the curriculum, a child needs to learn in order to feel confident about oneself. No wonder, "Education is the process of facilitating learning, or the acquisition of knowledge, skills, values, beliefs, and habits. Educational methods include teaching, training, storytelling, discussion and directed research. Education frequently takes place under the guidance of educators; however learners can also educate themselves. Education can take place in formal or informal settings and any experience that has a formative effect on the way one thinks, feels, or acts may be considered educational."[1]

In the words of Oscar Wilde Education is an admirable thing, but it is well to remember from time to time that nothing that is worth knowing can be taught.

The paper, as the title suggests, attempts to throw light on how student inclined teaching works create wonders in most cases. The student is vested with the power to think, ask questions, find answers and further reflect by sharing with the peers. Specially, in the case of language teaching, where the whole purpose lies in providing the learners opportunities and means to express in the target language, the method of "empowerment" takes an imperative role. To express oneself in a particular language, one needs to feel confident about the syntax, grammar as well as verbose in that particular language. The best way of achieving the same feeling is by consuming vernacular information in that language. That is the most naturally occurring way of one learning to understand and eventually express in a particular language. There isn't a better example to justify the aforementioned result, a newborn child learns one's mother tongue right from the day of birth, first by listening, trying to guess the meanings, sometimes misunderstands as well. Eventually, with passage of time, starts speaking and gets clearer on the misunderstandings and mistakes he or she has been making so far. This is all for the first language acquisition, it can be well assumed that the same method can aid in one's second language acquisition as well. This is the power of human mind's reasoning cognition that has a pivotal role in language learning. Yet time taking, but it is indeed an effective method of acquiring language, through the empowerment.

A general flow of language acquisition that sounds more pleasing than language teaching is through empowered learning. Students, if given the power to comprehend, reason, verify and apply their observations, can perform with much more confidence. To add, this way of learning allows them to assume a sense of creativity too. This is attributable to the fact that they believe in their ability to learn facts, derive signifying phenomena in the process of learning a language, if given the power and space to solve problems around.

Following are some ways of English consumption that get along well with the interest capturing of students.

Imaginative Comprehension

Various areas of the brain work together in a multitude of ways in order to produce the images that we see with our eyes and that are encoded by our brains. The basis of this work takes place in the visual cortex of the brain. The visual cortex is located in the occipital lobe of the brain and harbors many other structures that aid in visual recognition, categorization, and learning. One of the first things the brain must do when acquiring new visual information is recognize the incoming material. Brain areas involved in recognition are the inferior temporal cortex, the superior parietal cortex, and the cerebellum. During tasks of recognition, there is increased activation in the left inferior temporal cortex and decreased activation in the right superior parietal cortex. Recognition is aided by neural plasticity, or the brain's ability to reshape itself based on new information. Next the brain must categorize the material. The three main areas that are used when categorizing new visual information are the orbitofrontal cortex and two dorsolateral prefrontal regions which begin the process of sorting new information into groups and further assimilating that information into things that you might already know. After recognizing and categorizing new material entered into the visual field, the brain is ready to begin the encoding process – the process which leads to learning. Multiple brain areas are involved in this process such as the frontal lobe, the right extrastriate cortex, the neocortex, and again, the neostriatum. One area in particular, the limbic-diencephalic region, is essential for transforming perceptions into memories. With the coming together of tasks of recognition, categorization and learning; schemas help make the process of encoding new information and relating it to things you already know much easier. One can remember visual images much better when they can apply it to an already known schema. Schemas actually provide enhancement of visual memory and learning.

Multisensory realisation of facts ranging from vocabulary building to using full sentences in English is one of the most effective tools that help a learner grow in terms of language acquisition. Both in grammar as well as literature comprehension, if the pragmatic and working stage of the facts is shown and not just verbally told, it reaches one's long term memory that the following paragraph talks about.

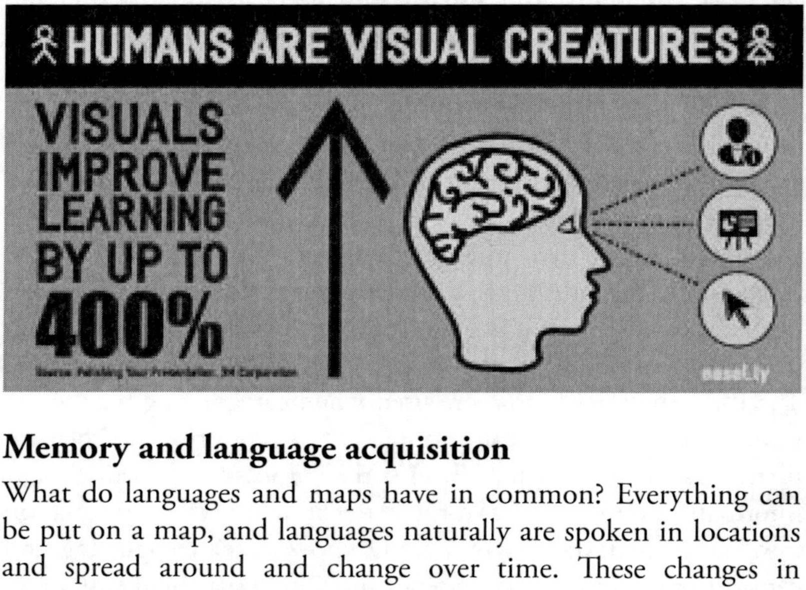

Memory and language acquisition

What do languages and maps have in common? Everything can be put on a map, and languages naturally are spoken in locations and spread around and change over time. These changes in pronunciations of words create a word history, or etymology. And by understanding how pronunciations change over time and where populations migrated, it's quite easy to remember a large number of data with just a memory map. This is how I anchor new languages I'm learning. I have a much bigger challenge when I try a new language family. So I look for even deeper and longer etymologies that are shared between language families, anything to help me establish a link to some core vocabulary. Some words like "I" (think

Old English "ic") and "me/mine" are essentially the same roots all over the world from Icelandic (Indo-European) to Finnish (Uralic) to Japanese (Altaic?) to Samoan (Austronesian).

From a polyglot telling the above experience, memory plays a highly imperative role in one's language development. From learning the basics, remembering the observations in one's surroundings pertains to the ramifications of "concrete learning". Our subconscious mind heroically pushes words and syntactical fames directly to our tongues while we try to converse or write in a language. Sometimes, one may have noticed, an unusual or to say, an unfamiliar word pops out of one's mouth at a very appropriate situation. Amazingly, it is nothing but the wonderfully functioning of the memory gland that might have grasped a word's function and suddenly when it was required to be used, it came out.

Same is the case how habits are correlated with language growth in an individual. One might be in a habit of using phrases such as "thank you" just by listening to surrounding people. No wonder, the first person could be entirely illiterate. That is the power of habits and the "basal ganglia". With habit and practice of using a language, a learner's concepts of sentence formation strengthen.

In an email conversation with Mr. Raghav Mehta, the Director of Talks For Change, he explained how his organisation works on the power of habits: "Talks For Change is an organization that endeavours to bring out the best in young children. It is initiated with an impetus to channelize the vigour and creativity that sometimes gets suppressed in children, subjective to distractions and tempting opportunities in the modern environment. Talks For Change deeply understands and empathises with the everyday challenges that school going generation feels in drawing productive actions that are nonetheless an eventuality arising out of their "habits". The power of habits is not unknown and we at Talks for Change have formulated effective as well as efficient tools that foster that particular key in one's growth, especially young children who are in the midst of crucial foundation stage of both their personal and professional establishment. Wise and intelligent decision making is one major catalyst in making of an influential personality that ultimately is a quality that comes with mastering one's habits. Talks For Change touches that root ingredient of a child's holistic enhancement, with an aim to making everyone believe in their own unique gifts so that every child works productively in achieving the best. The best way to define our concern for children is how Socrates expounds, "My friend, care for your psyche, know thyself, for once we know ourselves, we may learn how to care for ourselves."

Digital screening

> "Between the fall of 2012 and now, Google went from an interesting possibility to the dominant way that schools around the country" teach students to find information, create documents and turn them in, said Hal Friedlander, former chief information officer for the New York City Department of Education, the nation's largest school district. "Google established itself as a fact in schools."

Technology can support the effective execution of teaching strategies by promoting interaction, engagement and communication. Four in five (82%) educators agree that technology is a valuable tool for developing skills for the modern workplace. Technology is seen as most effective in enhancing the top teaching strategies for developing 21st century skills, as it can be used to promote interaction, engagement and collaboration.

Learning English is even easier in the era of digital monarchy. From the daily utility of a phone to connecting a Bluetooth speaker with the same, all require that one be accustomed to specific verbose of the digital world. Words like connect, delete, save, contacts, music, settings etc. have become so common that the basic vocabulary development is no more a challenge. Referring to CK Odgen's basic wordlist, one can thank technology for providing application based wordlist for an effortless English learning.

Illustrator, Ms. Richa Kinra states in her blog, "Children books are an essential part of every child's upbringing and they enjoy reading them or looking at their pictures. It is a fact that the children books intended for age group below 5 years are mainly dependent upon the illustrations, primarily because kids are more interested in looking at the illustrations and they have the capacity to imagine things and the pictures which help them imagine things and make them ask questions are a hit with them. Stories do play a very important role for kids above 5 years of age. Illustrations play important role in all kind of **children's books**. If you ever happen to ask any kid, what you like about a book the most, the reply will be the pictures or the illustrations. If you have done a lot of hard work thinking about the theme of the book and writing it, then you should keep in mind that illustrations will be equally important." She presses on the scope of pictorially representing literary works, "I have now illustrated more than 180 books and I have enjoyed each and every children book because there is so much to learn through these stories and also I get to know so much about various cultures and issues like child abuse, animal extinction, disability, mannerism issues etc."

Music as Mnemonics

A common criticism of mnemonics is that they only encourage rote memorization and do not help with higher order skills, such as comprehension or the transfer of knowledge. This criticism can be addressed with two responses. First, many mnemonics researchers (e.g., Bower, 1973; Higbee, 2001) have argued that mnemonics were designed to enhance recall, not facilitate higher order learning, and thus should be used as intended. Bower (1973) argued that although many teachers aspire for their students to be "critical, insightful, curious, and deeply appreciative of the subject matter" (p. 70), education still requires a great deal of fact learning, which mnemonics can help with. Learning basic facts with mnemonics leaves more time for higher order learning.

As an instance of music as a mnemonic, I tried to teach a group of children in the age range of eleven to thirteen, the use of 'did' in past tense. In order to make them factually remember the same, I composed a piece of "BeatBoxing" with the words-Did and Past.

Eventually, the beatbox composition was a hit in the whole school and kids couldn't get over the joy of learning the topic of tenses, seemingly a troublesome topic, in a joyful manner as such.

With respect to shared syntax and meaning processing in music and language, research suggests that the neurophysiological mechanisms responsible for syntax are enhanced, and develop earlier, due to musical training (Jentschke & Koelsch, 2009; Slevc, Rosenberg, & Patel, 2009). In addition, speech recognition and production depend on, and operate simultaneously with, conceptually-driven processes, such as awareness of the lexical, syntactic and semantic aspects of language (Rapp & Goldrick, 2000). Research suggests that two shared cognitive processes may underlie linguistic and musical syntax: working memory or executive functioning, and implicit learning (i.e., the ability to uncover an abstract structure from noisy input; Moreno et al., 2011; Francois & Schön, 2011). Although there is on-going research on the syntactic links between music and language (Slevc,

2012), no studies to date have been conducted to examine how music through these shared resources may influence the learning of L2 syntax and grammar. Due to the lack of studies regarding L2 structure and meaning aspects, this article discusses the available research on the potential phonological and reading benefits of musical experience on L2 learning.

Interview with a distinguished Special Educator, Mrs. Prem Bhayana, heading the Special Wing at OP Jindal Modern School, Hisar:

Question 1: What is the most important aspect of being a special educator?

Answer: There are two. Patience and creativity are the most significant prerequisites to becoming a good teacher not only in the field of special education but in general as well. Every person teaches us some or the other thing, intentionally or unintentionally, the most lasting lessons are those that seem interesting and useful to us.

Question: What do you do to make a lesson interesting and seem useful to a learner, especially in language learning?

Answer: Expressing oneself is the best gift to an individual, and children know them the best. Language learning becomes very interesting when we provide an outflow of information that appears not like a book chapter but a usual playtime activity.

Question: Kindly suggest some of your best working techniques in language teaching.

Answer: First we focus on environment building, it is followed by positive reinforcement of habits ranging from daily greeting to using new words, watching movies, playing sports, asking a lot of questions.

Question: Also, share your best practices in language learning to children with special needs.

Answer: All children fall in the category of having special needs. Every individual has a different set of cognition and reasoning pattern. As far as best practice is concerned, communicating is the best way of inducing language development in one's mind. Once a student starts using the language, we make sure that he or she improves with every spoken word spoken. Writing practice, spelling repetitions are a regular practice, again in an informal joyful manner. A student should feel excited for every lesson. Apart from playway methods, we encourage audiovisual ways of learning as gadgets have taken a glamorous place in children today. Games that empower children are a great source of imbibing strong conceptual clarity. Having pumped up with enthusiasm and eagerness, children take initiative to share their experiences and even compose stories. We follow chaining, modelling and shaping the potential of learners in order to make them curious to find out more and more to learn in language.

Works Cited

Bhayana, Prem. Personal Interview. 13 January 2020. https://ai.glossika.com/blog/memory-the-brain-and-language-acquisition

Campbell, Michael. "Relationship Between the Brain, Memory, and Language Learning". https://ai.glossika.com/blog/memory-the-brain-and-language-acquisition

Dewey, John (1944) [1916]. Democracy and Education. The Free Press. pp. 1–4. ISBN 978-0-684-83631-7.

Doyle, Latasha. "Visual Learning Statistics". 1 June 2017. https://www.easel.ly/blog/nycschoolstech-chat-resources-images/humans-visual-twitter-size-1/ Kinra, Richa. https://www.rksillustrations.com/

Lord, C. "Schemas and Images as Memory Aids: Two Modes of Processing Social Information". Stanford University. 1980. American Psychological Association.

Mehta, Raghav. "Re:Power oh Habits in Talks For Change Overview." Received by Garima Bhayana, 20 January. 2020.

Odgen, CK. Basic English: A General Introduction with Rules and Grammar. London: Paul Treber

Poldrack, R., Desmond, J., Glover, G., & Gabrieli, J. The Neural Basis of Visual Skill Learning: An fMRI Study of Mirror Reading. Cerebral Cortex. Jan/Feb 1998.

Putnam, Adam. (2015). Mnemonics in education: Current research and applications.. Translational Issues in Psychological Science. 1. 130-139. 10.1037/tps0000023 https://www.nytimes.com/2017/05/13/technology/google-education-chromebooks-schools.html

Singer, Natasha. "How Google Took Over the Classroom". The New York Times. May 13, 2017. https://www.nytimes.com/2017/05/13/technology/google-education-chromebooks-schools.html

Squire, L. Declarative and Nondeclarative Memory: Multiple Brain Systems Supporting Learning and Memory". 1992 Massachusetts Institute of Technology. Journal of Cognitive Neuroscience 4.3.

The Economist Intelligence Unit. The Economist. https://services.google.com/fh/files/misc/eiu_briefingpaper_jan2018.pdf

Vogel, R., Sary, G., Dupont, P., Orban, G. Human Brain Regions Involved in Visual Categorization. Elsevier Science (USA) 2002. "what kids learn today shapes the world we live in tomorrow" https://www.google.org/our-work/education/

"What kids learn today shapes the world we live in tomorrow" https://www.google.org/our-work/education/

Wikipedia. "Education". https://en.wikipedia.org/wiki/Education

Zeromskaite, I., 2014. The Potential Role of Music in Second Language Learning: A Review Article. Journal of European Psychology Students, 5(3), pp.78–88. DOI: http://doi.org/10.5334/jeps.ci

ground to begin working on mending low literacy rate- the first challenge one faces when teaching English. In this paper, I will talk about some of the methodologies I have used to create an immersive classroom environment for my students to help them develop and sustain an interest in learning. My research findings further relate the usage of sensory stimulation theory with an increase in Reading Comprehension levels of the students and increased attention span. Furthermore, the research points towards how visualization helps children in improving their basic grasp on concepts, learning new words, and helps them explore themes deeply. I would therefore argue that literature, when coupled with immersive pedagogy (such as sing-along lessons, play-acting, directed conversations in peer groups, etc.), can help strengthen techniques meant to increase classroom literacy levels that are often challenged by socio-economic factors the children face. It also inculcates a sense of self-expression, leadership, confidence in students.

The objective of this paper shall be to shed light on the methodologies through which literary tools are employed for the objective of building literary skills in children. These models of imparting education specifically target low resource government or low-income private schools and educational institutions in India. Due to the incongruent nature of growth in their formative years, children attending these schools face more difficulty in grasping communication skills in English language at school as compared to the children belonging to families who fall in the middle-income group. The paper shall first highlight some of the difficulties that children belonging to lower income groups face while studying in government schools, which not only impacts their personal growth during their foundational years, but also endangers their chances of securing employment in white collar jobs post senior secondary education. Researchers[1] have found that the schools which attempt to provide education to children belonging to lower income groups have generally been unable to produce good communication skills in English language. There is a critical need to strengthen basic levels of English comprehension in the classrooms. This inequity can be traced through a myriad number of reasons that range from very high student-teacher ratio in classrooms to employment of poorly trained teachers, from non-involvement of highly-equipped think tanks that focus on child psychology and school education to abject economic and social conditions in the community where most students studying in these schools dwell, and finally from abysmal resources within government schools to low motivation towards completing education. These children are usually first-generation learners in their families. This is also the reason why there is an absence of adults who can motivate and guide them through their studies. Moreover, the nature of the occupation of the parents in lower income groups is highly volatile and necessitates continuous movement from one place to another. In most of these cases, due to different educational policies in different states, and due to the challenges faced by families in the processes of displacement and relocation, children are unable to acquire sustained sense of education, as they are shifted from one school to another, and in many cases are even unable to secure an admission in another school. For instance, one of the students in my school in class VI has to leave school next month as his father, who is a driver by profession, recently lost his job. Although, this child is above the National RC target, he is compelled to discontinue his education (National RC refers to National reading Comprehension level).

It is also important to note that interpersonal skills and comprehension in English language in India has become crucial for securing popular well-paying jobs (for instance, BPOs, corporate jobs, secretarial positions, etc.), and in such cases, it becomes an immensely difficult task for these children to acquire soft skills so as to break the barrier of social economical class[2] constructs and secure financial security. As a result, their dreams and aspirations are compromised when it comes to facing the harsh realities of making a livelihood and even the brightest of minds succumb to this social barrier.

Teach for India's vision towards imparting an excellent education in government and low-income private schools involves developing student leadership as a way of empowering children by trying to help them find their voice. It intends to guide them into making fruitful life choices by helping them identify what they want to do in their life, by making them more aware of their surroundings, and by helping them become more invested in their communities as citizens of this country. These are some of the objectives that Teach for India has been striving to attain. I, as a Teach for India fellow, try to help children assert their voices and articulate themselves by creating a safe space, where children and fellows are considered equal partners in the process of learning. Experience informs us that with the intervention by Teach for India, children have developed a sense of appreciation and respect for themselves and others around them. They have also gained skills pertaining to deep reflection and critical thinking. Moreover, they have also formed affective connections with children belonging to junior grades whom they often offer to mentor.

Now that I have briefly highlighted the socio-economic context of these children, the role that Teach For India plays in addressing solutions to the educational crisis that low-income private and governmental schools are facing, and the environment that I, as a fellow, am trying to create in my classroom, I will now proceed to explain the methodologies, I have been deploying in my classroom to build literary awareness and English Reading Comprehension levels. I teach English and Social Science to a class of 38 students at Navayug School, Moti Bagh, Delhi, and the observations that follow are based on my teaching experience in the same class.

Sensory Stimulation Theory

Children are excellent observers, and when guided, they are capable of taking note of their surroundings in a manner that enhances their critical thinking. In our classrooms, we focus on how children can learn concepts, as well articulate their opinions, instead of simply reading or learning what has been presented in front of them or prescribed to them. In this study, I focus on the deployment of Sensory Stimulation Theory and Visualization and how it helps to drive the immersive learning experience of literature for the students.

The central conceptual framework of Sensory stimulation theory involves a stimulation of senses in order to accentuate effective learning[3]. According to Laird[4], "Sensory stimulation theory is based on that people best learn when the senses are stimulated" (1985). Laird in his research found that "majority of learning occurred through sense, namely seeing (75%), hearing (13%) and smelling, touching and tasting (12%)". In the classroom, for instance, while teaching the poem "Beauty" by E-Yeh-Shure, I took my class to the school ground and asked them to close their eyes and hear the chirruping of the birds and feel the fragrance of the flowers and breathe in the clear sky. I then asked them if they felt beauty within. The children liberated themselves from their preoccupations and in retrospective silence, appreciated what was around them while also understanding the theme of the poem "Beauty".

Reinforcement theory, as developed by Burrhus Frederic, "believed that positive reinforcement, whether verbal such as "well done" or more tangible such as certificate or promotion in an organisation will improve people learning". However, Burrhus Frederic also stated "that negative reinforcement such as punishment will also improve people learning". In teach for India, methodologies such as Positive behaviour narration cycle and reflection as a technique of behaviour management cycle are followed, that instead of punishing a child, involve introspection on the part of the child. Positive behaviour narration also involves improving a child's morale by citing good behaviour on the part of their peers and then expressing the desire of the instructor for a child to follow the similar approach to ensure good behaviour. For instance, in my classroom if a child does not pay attention, I usually tell the child, "I really like how Deepali is listening to the speaker; I would really appreciate if Suraj were to do the same".

Visualization

Visualization as a process helps in creating mental images of what is being taught and in developing rich experiences so as to make connections. Through the technique of Visualization, children are able to affectively connect with the subject being taught. For instance, while teaching the poem "Vocation" by Rabindranath Tagore, which highlights the curiosity in a child going to school by observing different people occupied with their chores, I asked the children to imagine themselves to be in the position of the hawker, the bangle seller, the watchman and the gardener. Through this process, children in the classroom were then asked to act like they belonged to these occupations, thus instilling an empathetic understanding of the vocation. In this way, children were able to dismantle the binaries of self and other, and consequently, de-stigmatized the biases associated with certain occupations. Harrison Barnes talks about the school that Albert Einstein attended as a child, which followed the teaching methods of the Swiss educator Johann Pestalozzi. The schools established by Pestalozzi taught children through the techniques of the Pestalozzi Method (the "Method"). This method "believed that instead of dealing with words, children should learn through activity and objects. They should be free to pursue their own interests and reach their own conclusions". The text *How Gertrude Teaches Her Children*, written by Pestalozzi in 1801 sheds light on several teaching methodologies that departed from the conventional modes of imparting education. His work "discusses the importance of spontaneity and allows children to arrive at answers themselves". Visualization featured as a crucial component in the methodologies formulated by Pestalozzi, who"believed that visualization was among the mind's most powerful features and that imagery was where all knowledge started". The application of Pestalozzi's methodologies deeply impacted Einstein's experience at school. His biography, *Einstein: His Life and Universe*, written by Walton Isaacson, mentions that "it was a perfect school for Einstein. The teaching was based on encouraging students to visualize images…The visual understanding of concepts, as stressed by Pestalozzi and his followers, became a significant aspect of Einstein's genius". "Visual understanding is the essential and only true means of teaching how to judge things correctly," Pestalozzi wrote, and "the learning of numbers and language must be definitely subordinated." Einstein believed that visual understanding was the most important form of education and more important than knowledge."

In my lesson plans, I introduce hypothetical situation that are conducive for the children to experience what is being taught by pushing them to explore how it feels to be actually present in the scenario.

The following excerpt has been taken from my lesson plan in which my objective was to make the students aware of the ongoing Australian Bushfire. To begin with, I displayed an image of a kangaroo running in a burning Australian forest and asked them to imagine what immediate feelings they experienced if they were to imagine themselves as that kangaroo. They were then asked the following questions:

- Imagine yourself to be the kangaroo in this picture.
- What do you smell, touch, hear, feel right now?
- What are you running from?
- How are you feeling right now?

The students answered these questions vividly with moving expressions describing close the experience of what according to their imagination the situation must feel like. Of course, the children cannot entirely experience what the people and animals facing the crisis have undergone or are going through. However, by visualizing themselves in a similar situation, they are able to bridge that gap, and thereby also become more cognizant to the effects of climate change and the need to conserve the environment. They were then introduced to the possible ways one might act for their survival, what causes such disasters, and how can they be managed. Exercises like these also help the students develop empathy, and thus make connections to the core values of the lesson objective.

While introducing new words and their meanings, the students are asked to pay attention to how the words sound and what do they immediately make them think? They are also asked to feel how their tongues roll while pronouncing those words. If a word like "Rough" is spoken, it is snappy and causes a force on the upper palate with the tongue, while a word like "Glib" is makes the tongue slip smoothly through the teeth. If the objective of the lesson includes a skill like "Examine", then it has to be broken down for the kids to understand. To examine something, first it needs to be seen, heard or felt. Then the information about the topic has to be recalled. A connection has to be established between the previous information and the new observation. Then the relationship needs to be studied and concluded. Comparing the Reading Comprehension level of the children from the Beginning of Year assessment to the End of Year assessment, to the Middle of Year Assessment, majority of students witnessed an increase in Reading Comprehension levels. Learning in schools are highly based on stimulating hearing and visual senses, but if all the senses could be deployed learning can be increased in multifold.

Conclusion

The processes of Visualization and Sensory Stimulation Learning theory highlighted above are deeply interconnected with each other. Stimulating the senses in visualization makes the process an immersive experience. Both complement each other to create a rich and rigorous understanding of a given concept. With the deployment of sensory pedagogy, students become more reflective about understanding of the world around them, their schools, localities and the city. The scope of critical thinking consequently becomes more expansive, as the teacher discusses various systems and institutions that sustain the functioning of a society. For instance, I organize periodic class discussions and debates before assigning the roles of class monitors. To make the process more democratic, I divide the class into groups and ask each of them to put forward a representative via internal voting. Those representatives then discuss and participate in the management of class activities. I also conduct mock debates following a mini-Parliament model wherein we discuss the themes encountered in their lessons. Through such activities, students become much more vocal, active, and aware. This engagement also helps them develop leadership skills.

There are also some students in my class who find it challenging to participate actively in class, or to coherently articulate their thoughts. In such cases, I conduct special classes with the help of volunteers, where we have developed a non-pressurizing, non-competitive space of shared learning. I make pairs of two and assign them simple yet action-oriented tasks that aim at vocalization of ideas. These tasks range from voice modulation, poetry recitation, self-definition, one-act play, and improvisation.

Moreover, our organization conducts monthly Learning Circle meetings for the fellows to share and engage with each other's experiences in the classroom. Although we face similar challenges as teachers, our understanding of how to formulate our teaching methodologies becomes specific and individualistic. For this reason, experts from the field of education and child psychology are often brought on board by the organization to guide the fellows in customizing their lesson plans according to the needs of the class. Program Managers are also assigned the task to visit each school to observe and supervise the fellows on their teaching. To conclude, I believe that this kind of immersive framework builds the foundation of a socially productive mindset in the classroom. It inculcates a sense of awareness and appreciation towards what students are surrounded by. It is the zeal to protect and promote this culture of understanding is what sustains the essence of literature, inventive thought, and creative expression.

Works Cited

https://philosophyessays.net/sensory-stimulation-theory-of-learning/

https://www.harrisonbarnes.com/einstein-visualization-and-your-career/

Notes

1. Data on schools comparing educational level, results of governmental schools and private schools. While the results have improved due to current governmental initiatives, they still are below the general statistics of pass percentages of private schools. Source Outlook.
2. Data shown by Asia Society highlights the economic disparity
3. https://www.ukessays.com/essays/education/the-sensory-stimulation-theory-education-essay.php.
4. See Laird, *Approaches to Training and Development.* 1985.

6

Going Beyond the Textbooks: Using Proverbs in English Class

— *Dr. Meena Sehrawat*

1. Introduction

It is high time when we understand that proper study of language does not only imply communicative competence and communicative proficiency, it also means having a proper understanding of the society. Teaching and learning of English can remain meaningful if it is properly Indianised; Indianised in terms of social relevance. In other words, in the Indian context, there is a greater need to emphasise on the contemporary Indian society; that is one must take into account the specific regional and cultural constituents without which teaching and learning of English would not be so authentic.

To make the teaching learning of literature more meaningful and language oriented, we need to modify our approach to teaching learning of literature. There is no denial of the fact that literature can very effectively be used to provide learners with rich vocabulary or syntactic items. It can be used to help students learn various characteristics of the written language, the sentence structures and patterns, skill to connect and express ideas in an influential way and finally develop and enrich their own writing skills. This way literature can effectively be used to improve their communicative and cultural competence.

However, Literature is not only what we conveniently call story, poem, autobiography or whatsoever name we give to the written form. Literature is all around us. It may also exist in oral form. The English studies in the contemporary context will enrich our understanding, if we care to extend the conventional boundary and include the proverbs which we find around us in every region we live in. These proverbs, which are at finger tips of the people living in a particular region, provide a window to the socio-cultural context of that particular region, in addition to encapsulating the basic human truth.

Adedimeji (2005) defines proverb as a short familiar sentence expressing a supposed truth or moral lesson. It is simple, popular, frequently used but it also requires explanation. Another prominent proverb scholar Mieder (1993) also considers proverbs as a short, generally known sentence of folk which contains wisdom, truth, moral and traditional views in a metaphorical, fixed and memorized form, easy to be handed down from generation to generation. Obviously, the study of proverbs can also help lend that element of interest and bonding to the study of English studies which is sadly missing in today's teaching.

2. The Current scenario

2.1. Issues in Question

- Let's begin with some issues in question:
- Why do our schools, especially, government schools fail to develop the communicative competence among the students'?
- Why the two skills listening and speaking are ignored while teaching English?
- Why do we feel that completing English textbook means, the syllabus is completed?

- What can be done to ensure the learners' involvement?
- How can we focus more on listening and speaking skills?

It's a very serious concern that despite the mushroom growth of the so-called English schools in the country at the popular demand of English from class 1, the craze for the language and literature is on wane at the school level. Do we need to teach English only as a subject or do we really want to have proper command over the language to delve deep into the ocean of literature that this language offers and develop communicative competence? It may also be the reason that at the lower level it is not the choice of the children but the choice of parents thrust upon them.

2.2. Major causes

Some of the major causes that have led to current state of stagnancy in terms of teaching language and literature at the school level include:

- The listening speaking skills at schools are neglected. Even the examination system is hardly bothered to assess these skills. Curriculum needs to be updated in these lines at all levels i.e. at primary, middle, secondary and senior secondary. Though, at senior secondary level CBSE had started ASL (Assessment of Speaking & Listening). This sort of intervention is required at all levels.
- Hardly any attempt to ensure skills, which could meet the needs and aspirations of the learners; e.g. to acquire English to deal with real situations. The school lacks this vision.
- No attempt to link classroom teaching with the life outside: the teaching learning in the classroom remains delinked and dissociated from the life outside.
- Emphasis on information gathering and cracking the exams rather than on understanding and ability to apply the same in real life situation.

2.3. Some ways to improve the situation

The need of the hour is to make the teaching learning process interesting, useful and relevant for the learners. The course needs to be designed as such that it catches the fancy of the learners. The teachers too need to be innovative in their classes. Some ways which can help in this regard include:

- Affinity with text: selection of the text and the subsequent exploitation - moving beyond the text.
- Use of simple technology - Use of technology or smart phones by the teacher can be useful in the classroom to make the teaching learning process interesting as well as relevant for the learners. Teacher can form a WhatsApp group and share audios and videos for listening and reading exercises, which can further be discussed in the classroom. In fact, incorporating latest technologies in teaching both language and literature is the need of the hour. The internet could prove to be an invaluable source in a learner participatory teaching approach, in which teachers would become equal participants in learning and help the independent investigation of the learners towards their desired goal. Similarly, the multimedia would lend a great help in developing the listening and speaking skills of the learners. (Amit Narula:2012)
- Folk tale/ folk lore: folk literature can be exploited at the school level as well and this will help connect the learners to their society.
- Using popular proverbs in mother tongue / regional languages/ dialects: this will be immensely useful at all levels and this is the focus of the present paper.

3. What is proverb and why should proverbs be included in English Class?

3.1. What is a proverb?

Proverbs have been defined differently by different scholars engaged in language teaching or researchers. Harnish (1993) defines proverb as a short familiar maxim of wisdom words which is usually expressed in form with bold image that catches the memory. Moriss (2003) looks upon proverb as a brief, pithy statement or saying, which is in constant and widespread use and presents a truth or fact. Hornby (2010) views proverb as a well-known sentence or phrase that gives advice that is generally true. Norrick (1985) focuses on the literary nature of the proverbs. In his view, literary proverbs on the one hand are rich in figures of speech especially metaphors, and on the other hand, they are remarkable for alliteration and rhythm.

3.2. Why should proverbs be included in English Class?

Proverbs should be made an integral component of language teaching - be it the home language or the second language; simply because they are the traditional (historic) sayings of a society. Proverbs are short, clever sentences, encapsulating the experiences of several generations; hence they usually offer rich life advice. Proverbs have immense potentiality to spread knowledge, wisdom and truths about life. Hence, they can play an important role in language teaching, especially in terms of gaining cultural knowledge, metaphorical understanding and communicative competence. The fact that native speakers often use them very naturally in conversation without even realizing, it confirms this claim. The learners will be comfortable with the proverbs they have been using or listening in the locality; hence the sense of fear which is one of the most fatal obstacles to learning a language like English can very effectively be mitigated. This will be possible because such a strategy will bring teaching close to the learners' life and there will be a great opportunity for the teachers to exploit the mother tongue as a rich resource for teaching / learning English.

The usefulness of Proverbs in teaching can also be assessed on the ground of their rich cultural content. They reveal about the culture of a society more than any textbook. And language teaching is not only teaching about the language or the proper usage of linguistic items, it also implies teaching manners and instilling a sense of appropriateness. The use of proverbs can be of immense help in this regard. Proverbs can also make the people realise what is considered good behaviour and what is bad behaviour, what practices are good and what are not. This too is an important aspect of teaching in general and language teaching in particular.

Proverbs can also help us understanding the history of a place. What we need to do is to make a linguistic analysis of the words used. For example, proverbs from rural area with agricultural background will extensively use the words used in farming. Similarly, proverbs from the community that thrives on fishing will use the terms used in or related to fishing.

Proverbs can play a significant role in teaching English as a second language for effective communication (Ajoke, A. Hasan, K & Suleiman, Y.: 2015) especially in terms of building up vocabulary, illustrating the phraseology and idiomatic expressions of both the native and the non-native language. It consumes very little time'.

The study of classical literature should no doubt continue but contemporary literature especially the pieces that help create socio-cultural contexts should also be suitably incorporated as this would encourage learners participate actively in understanding and create appropriate communicative practices.

As has been stated earlier literature is all around us and English studies in the contemporary context will enrich our understanding if we care to extend the conventional boundary and include the proverbs which we find around us in every region we live in.

3.3. What sort of proverbs

As stated earlier, the proverbs and sayings sum up the social and historical experiences of the people. Hence, all sorts of proverbs can and should easily be used in the class.

These proverbs are passed on from one generation to the next as readymade utterances and they also pass on the prejudices and apprehensions of one generation to another. The students would love to have inkling into the changing perceptions of the society about particular castes, gender or region and the social customs. So the language study would have interesting blending with the socio-culture study.

3.4: Some Effective Ways used to bring Proverbs in the Classroom:

- Encouraging learners to tell popular proverbs: Learners were asked to tell the proverbs which they often listen to. The proverb used at their homes or in surroundings in their day to day conversations and then in the class they find its English equivalent.
- Encouraging them to explain when do they use a particular proverb (context)
- Inviting them to explain the meaning or tell, why they use it in a particular context. Finding its contextual relevance provided them a window to the socio-cultural context of that particular region in addition to encapsulating the basic human truth.
- Leading them to a discussion over the meaning – then and now (cultural studies). We found that some of the proverbs which were based on caste gave them the insight about various caste systems in India and also revealed how they form the basis of a culture of resistance and how as inherited wisdom, they figuratively refer to the socio-cultural context of the contemporary society.
- Proverb interpretation used as a contest and declaring a winner of the class.
- Translation of English proverbs into their mother tongue as an assignment: Learners were asked to translate some of the proverbs into their mother tongue with the help of adults at home. While translating in their mother tongue, it was found that though they were translated in the different mother tongues such as in Punjabi, Bhojpuri, Maithali, Bengali, Haryanvi dialect, Poorvi UP dialect but their meaning or context was the same. They realised that though the proverbs had different languages and different state specific context but their meaning is same i.e. Unity in Diversity. The cross currents of various cultures transmitted

through various languages is very strong and together they make the rich cultural heritage of India. This helped the learners to find some substantial links between different states, the life around them and what is being taught in the classroom. The use of proverbs served this purpose to a great extent.

- Used Proverbs in the classroom as a password: It was decided that the class is going to have a password of the day and it would be a proverb. Whosoever comes into the classroom will say the password of the day. This was told to them in the first period. Suppose someone forgets the password, then the penalty was that they will be told the password but then they will have to frame a sentence on it. This exercise was done for about a month. Initially, teacher told them a proverb as a password but later on they themselves decided the password. In this way lot of proverbs with their meaning and sentences were in their bank of active vocabulary. For example, the password was: It's better to be safe than sorry. Meaning: It's better to be cautious than regret later. One of the sentences framed on it was: I asked my father to drive with a seat belt when he was dropping me to the school because it is **better to be safe than sorry**.

  There were many such examples which showed that they are not only using the proverbs in their classroom but also in their day to day life.
- Used in Language Games and Activities: Some games and activities were developed to learn and use them with fun such as:

Whisper down the Secret

Procedure:

1. Each row of students' was made one team; there were five rows so five teams.

2. Student sitting on the last bench was called out and a proverb was whispered in their ear.
3. Then starting from the back of the class the proverb was whispered to the last student in each row.
4. Then they passed it on quietly so that the others do not hear.
5. They, in turn, must repeat it to the person in front of them, and so on.
8. The student in the front of each row then wrote down what he or she heard.
9. The team with most accurate proverb in less time was declared the winner.

Let's Draw and Check:

Procedure:

1. The class was divided in five groups.
2. A slip of paper with a proverb written on it was given to each group.
3. They were asked to frame correct and meaningful sentence on it.
4. Then they were asked to draw the picture depicting that proverb.
5. After completing the picture they were asked to show it to the class. If the groups were able to identify the proverb then they got 1 mark.
6. The group that drew well with a correct sentence was the winner

- Writing stories using lot of proverbs: Students were divided in groups and then asked to write a story using proverbs. Before writing the story the rubrics for assessing the story was discussed.

  This also helped them to self assess their story and their use of sentence structures, patterns, proverbs and creativity.

It hones their skill to connect and express ideas in an influential way and finally develop and enrich their own writing skills. In this way, literature can effectively be used to improve their communicative and cultural competence.

- Writing stories based on any proverb: As an assignment, they were asked to write stories on any of the proverb, keeping in mind the criteria, used in the rubrics discussed and used in the group work of writing a story. But this time they used any single proverb.

Conclusion

Using Proverbs as a strategy in the English classroom can be very effective in terms of introducing the elements of interest in and bonding with the subject. This can help dispel the environment of boredom. The proverbs can be used for the variety of purposes in the English class. For instance, they can be used to teach vocabulary – to give the learners a feel how words have different meanings in different associations. So they can be made aware of the denotative and connotative implications of the words. The proverbs can be very effective also in developing the skill of social interaction for the simple reason that proverbs belong to the traditional verbal folklore genre, and the proverbs carry wisdom with them that people often use during social interaction all over the world. Besides, they are concise, easy to remember and useful in every situation in life. Used judiciously, English proverbs are expected to improve learners' vocabulary learning Mieder, (1985). Besides building vocabulary, Proverbs can be used as very effective and practical tools to exemplify and practice grammar, pronunciation and creative use of the language. Proverbs can be useful also in enhancing fluent and natural language production (Yorio, 1980) ability of the learners. So, going beyond the textbook and using proverbs in English class can really help learners to master the language skills.

The use of proverbs as suggested here, is in tune with Amit Narula's word of advice: People have realized that in this globalised world, English is a language of opportunity, and, if for the average Indian it is difficult to adapt to the American or British standard, then the next best thing would be to make the language adapt to the country and people. (Amit Narula:2012)

Works Cited

Adedimeji, M.A. (2005). Logical Fallacies and Thirty English Proverbs: A Truth Conditional Semantic Approach. The Abuja Communicator.(2) 1. pp. 122 – 143.

Ajoke, A. Hasan, K & Suleiman, Y. (2015). Examining the Use of Proverbs in Teaching English as Second Language: An Implication for Secondary School Principals in Nigeria. ELT VIBES: International E-Journal For Research in ELT. 1(3), 14-28.

Harnish (1993), Robert M. (1993) "Communicating with Proverbs". Communication and coignition. Monographies (26 (30-4): 265-290 (1993)

Hornby, A. S. (2010). Oxford advanced learners dictionary of current English. 8th ed. London: Heinemann.

Mieder, W. (1985) Popular Views of the Proverb. Proverbium: Yearbook of International Proverb Scholarship, 2, 109-143.

Mieder, Wolfgang (1993". Proverbs Are Never Out of Season. Popular Wisdom in the Modern Age. New York: Oxford University Press.

Narula, Amit (2012) "English in A Globalized World" www.thecriterion. com The Criterion: An International Journal in English ISSN 0976-8165 Vol. III. Issue. I 1 March 2012)

Norrick, Neal (1985), How proverbs mean: Semantic studies in English proverbs. Berlin: Mouton.

Yorio, C.A (1980).Conventionalized language forms and the development of communicative competence. TESOL Quarterly, 14(4), pp. 433-442.

Web Resources

- Hindimeaning.com
- Scoopwhoop.com

7

Improving Reading Skills of Students of Class Two in English through Innovative Practices

— *Dr. Khaleeq Ahmad & Richa Chahal*

A conscious teacher, somewhere in the national capital of New Delhi, who was teaching English to the students of class two realised that reading as a skill, {*"the process of looking at a series of written symbols and getting* Meaning from them"... while *receiving written symbols (letters, punctuation marks and spaces) we use our brain to convert them into words, sentences and paragraphs, (slightly adapted from englishclub.com)*} of students in English was not being improved, as per the desired inclination of the teacher. What she taught and expected was not being achieved in the reading of English language. The learning objectives were not met. She was concerned of the fact that the reading skills in English of the students of class two were not up to the mark. There was no expected fluency level in the reading of English in her class. This self-realisation of the teacher motivated and led her to do something in this area. She contacted a comparatively senior & experienced teacher who has been doing action research earlier also and who could not only guide her in this study but also be the part of the study. The two of them decided to take this small action research as a case study on the premise that "***students' reading skills were not being enhanced as per the desired outcomes in English and that the skills could be improved by adopting certain innovative practices***". As Mission Buniyaad had already been launched in India which was a three-month campaign, "Under the scheme, the government will work towards ensuring that all children… are able to read and write Hindi and do basic Mathematics in the next three months. The mission was launched after the National Achievement Survey (NAS) found that majority of students did not perform well in science, mathematics and languages, (adapted) {https://www.google.com/amp/s/www.thehindu.com/news/cities/Delhi/mission-buniyaad-launched/article23506965.ece/amp/} This Mission mainly focused on enhancing the reading skills of students in Hindi language. The Mission actually inspired and awakened the teacher to experiment with something similar in English. She also felt that it was the need of the hour to develop students' reading skills in English, as it is taught as the second language in school. The two researchers unanimously decided to adopt some innovative or hitherto less tried practices in only one particular section of class two so that, later on, the progress could be compared with the other section of the same class and other primary classes which were being taught with the same conventional and routine methods. This one section was chosen in order to fathom the comparative effect of the strategies adopted at a later stage.

It was also decided that these innovative practices of improving reading skills would be used in the selected section for three months continuously and after three months the progress of the group of learners would be discreetly assessed and compared with the progress of the group of learners from the other section. It was also decided that if they were successful in achieving the desired results i.e. improve the reading skills of students of class two in English, these practices would be implemented in other section(s) and other classes too, if possible.

Both, before and after the study, a baseline or placement discreet test of the target group of students was decided to be conducted, therefore, the students, before the beginning of the study were observed through the simple reading tool and marked on their levels of learning, as was done in Hindi under Mission Buniyaad. On the basis of their reading skills in English these students were placed in any of the following three levels of learning in that class. These three levels were decided to be-

(a) **Alphabet Level**- In this level the reader identifies the alphabet but is unable to make any letter and sound connections and read the whole word. Sometimes, the learner can read the word with difficulty.

(b) **Word Level**- The reader of this level is the reader who has learned that letters and sounds are related. The reader uses the beginning and ending sounds to try and pronounce words while reading the text but cannot read a phrase or sentence in continuation.

(c) **Sentence Level**- Finally, the reader, at this level, enters the sentence stage, where he can identify whole words instantly and recurring letter patterns become noticeable by the reader (Linnea C. Ehri, 1987) and goes on to read phrases in a row with some fluency.

Within these three levels, students were expected to develop the recognition of familiar and unfamiliar words and that they would be able to read and advance towards the whole sentence or at least to the next level with some fluency."Fluency is defined as the ability to read with speed, accuracy, and proper expression. In order to understand what they read, children must be able to read fluently whether they are reading aloud or silently. When reading aloud, fluent readers read in phrases and add intonation appropriately. (https://www.readingrockets.org/helping/target/fluency)

Since, it was now decided to conduct the study with the students to improve their reading skills and increase their level of reading in English, tools were required to be developed. The following two strategies were decided to be adopted continuously for three months in order to increase the reading level of one section of class two-

(a) Word Wall

(b) Rhyming words (including jazz chants)

Word Wall- a "wall dedicated to display high frequency words (these could be sight words or words that appear frequently in your text) that are important for your students to know and use" (https://www.weareteachers.com/what-is-a-word-wall/) for example, the words 'at', 'on', 'that', 'it, 'they', 'this' etc. are considered high frequency words in class two. The main purpose of a word wall is to help students build sight word recognition, so that they can recognize and read them at a glance. In primary classes, two to four high frequency words are added daily to word wall until there are between 110 to 120 words (ibid). Utilising word walls may help students develop a sight word vocabulary that further allows them to retain the words and read text (Hall & Cunningham, 1999). When students are able to retrieve the words from long-term memory, they can become more fluent (Ehri, 2005) and achieve success in reading. The words are written with thick black marker or coloured paper and are placed on the wall. Students practice new and old words each day by looking at them, clapping, chanting, snapping the letters, writing the words on paper and self-correcting the words with the teacher. Teacher may also use these words to focus on spellings (Reading Horizons Volume 49 Issue 4 November/December 2009 Article 5 11-2009). It is an interactive tool for students and contains an array of words that can be used while reading. Word wall provides a permanent model for high frequency words. It helps students to understand the patterns and relationships of words and in building reading skills. (https://learningstrategieseng491.weebly.com/word-wall.html)

Rhyming words help learners notice and work with the sounds within a word. Being able to break words into smaller parts and recognise smaller parts in words (Bradley, L., & Bryant, P. E.) is an important skill required for reading and learning spelling. Rhyming also let children learn to read about the patterns and structures of language. Rhyming is important to reading because it can help children to understand that words that share common sounds often share common letter sequences. So if you can spell cat, you can also spell hat, rat, and mat. While learning a rhyme, learners learn to anticipate the rhyming words. The learners will be able to make predictions of forthcoming words while reading (http://www.ascd.org/publications/books/103316/chapters/Readiness-Phonemic-Awareness.aspx_).

These two strategies were to be adopted by the teacher of class two for three months to develop reading skills and study the implications.

Now, the researcher-teacher began teaching of English through these two techniques to enhance the reading skills of students in the month of April in addition to other traditional techniques.

Forty students of class two in the school, where English is taught as a second language became the part of this study. The students were seven and eight years old, with different reading levels based upon the discreet observation made by the teacher as described above. Read-aloud, shared reading, paired reading and independent reading, were regular activities in the class already in place. In addition to them, students were encouraged to use the word wall and rhyming words to build their reading skills and achieve a considerable level of fluency in reading.

In the word wall activity, selected and frequently occurring words in the text book were taken up, written on chart papers with the help of students and these chart papers were pasted on the wall. The learners were given specific time slots to visit the wall, read the words aloud and use them in sentences in their groups. Teacher helped them in recognising, decoding, pronouncing, repeating and drilling the words on the wall with the help of the white board. Gradually, more number of words were added to the word wall to make the learners comfortable with reading new words and recycling the previously owned words.

"Researchers first discovered the relation between rhyming and reading in the 1980s. Since then, study after study has suggested that good rhymers turn out to be good readers". (Learning Liftoff,

Jun 26, 2015). Rhyming word activities proved quite beneficial in raising the levels of reading skill of these girls. There was a lot of fun with words while rhyming words were taken up. The students enjoyed a lot in making pairs of similar ending sound words and also created their own sense and non-sense rhymes. These rhyming words were also ultimately taken to and merged with the word wall and retained them for three months thus integrating the two techniques to improve the reading skills of the students. Jazz Chants, in the process of introducing rhyming words, were also taken, and these chants helped a lot as these proved to be a rhythmic expression of language for the students to enjoy their English class. Jazz Chants "are Carolyn Graham's snappy, upbeat chants and poems that use jazz rhythms to illustrate the natural stress and intonation patterns of conversational American English." {from, Oxford University Press, available at-

https://www.google.com/url?sa=t&source=web&rct=j&url=https://www.scribd.com/doc/148999973/What-is-the-Meaning-of-Jazz-Chant&ved=2ahUKEwiR4auwlPXjAhVQT30KHR1ICVcQFjAbegQICRAB&usg=AOvVaw3nM-73XxZZypQgfxHpq1di}. Jazz chants are instrumental in introducing readers to rhythm, stress and grouping. {Adapted, (Source- https://skyteach.ru/2019/03/03/jazz-it-up-teaching-english-with-jazz-chants/}

The jazz chant of three popular rhymes which were not the part of their syllabus included

(a) Johnny, Johnny, yes papa
(b) Ba ba black sheep
(c) Rain, rain go away

Repetitions, drilling, jazz chant and chorus singing of these rhymes considerably helped the researchers in enhancing the reading skills of students in English with fun, joy and excitement.

Data analysis/ Results & Findings

As mentioned earlier, the students were assessed discreetly, in a non-threatening manner before the beginning and after the completion of study. Their levels of learning in the beginning of the study were, as follow-

Total strength of the class = 40
Alphabet level - 14/40
Word level - 21/40
Sentence level - 05/40

After three months the students were again discreetly assessed and the findings are as follow-

Total strength of the class = 40
Alphabet level - 06/40
Word level - 18/40
Sentence level - 16/40

Though, there were six students still standing at the 'alphabet level', yet it was also to be noticed that eight students had moved forward to the next level i.e. word level. At this level also, i.e. word level, before the beginning of the study there were 21 students but, now, after three months, 18 students remained at this level as compared to the situation earlier i.e. 21. The biggest achievement of all this exercise and action research was observed at the sentence level where, the total number of students increased from five to sixteen. It was a jump of more than 200%, which was quite surprising even for the researchers, and this gave them a feeling of moral boosting and self-satisfaction.

Thus, the premise and the hypothesis that the reading skills of the students in class two could be enhanced by adopting techniques like word wall and rhyming words including jazz chants proved valid. Students had real fun while they learnt. Their reading speed gradually increased; and interestingly they didn't even notice this fact. Many of them very enthusiastically confided that it was joy to study that way and that they wanted to study the same way in future too. Later, it was decided that these techniques would be adopted in other section and classes too where many students were stagnant at the alphabet level.

Works Cited

Bradley, L., & Bryant, P. E. (1983). Categorizing sounds and learning to read—A causal connection. Nature, 301, 419-421.

Ehri, L. (2005). Learning to read words: Theory, findings, and issues. Scientific Studies of Reading, 9(2), 167-188.

Englishclub.com available at https://www.englishclub.com/reading/what.htm

Hall, D., & Cunningham, P. (1999). Multilevel word study — Word charts, word walls, and word sorts. In I. Fountas & G. Pinnell (Eds.), Voices on Word Matters —Learning about Phonics and Spelling in the Literacy Classroom (pp.114-130). Portsmouth, NH: Heinemann.

http://www.ascd.org/publications/books/103316/chapters/Readiness~Phonemic-Awareness.aspx_

https://learningstrategieseng491.weebly.com/word-wall.html

https://www.readingrockets.org/helping/target/fluency

https://skyteach.ru/2019/03/03/jazz-it-up-teaching-english-with-jazz-chants/

https://www.google.com/amp/s/www.thehindu.com/news/cities/Delhi/mission-buniyaad-launched/article23506965.ece/amp/

https://www.google.com/url?sa=t&source=web&rct=j&url=https://www.scribd.com/doc/148999973/What-is-the-Meaning-of-Jazz-Chant&ved=2ahUKEwiR4auwlPXjAhVQT30KHR1ICVcQFjAbegQICRAB&usg=AOvVaw3nM-73XxZZypQgfxHpq1di}

Learning Liftoff, Jun 26, 2015, (available at https://www.learningliftoff.com/take-the-time-to-rhyme-how-rhyming-benefits-early-education/)

Linnea C. Ehri (1987) LEARNING TO READ AND SPELL WORDS, University of California, School of Education, Davis, CA 9561, article published in Journal of Reading Behavior 1987, Volume XIX, No. 1.

Reading Horizons Volume 49 Issue 4 November/December 2009 Article 5 11-2009 The Effects of Word Walls and Word Wall Activities on the Reading Fluency of First Grade Students Joanne Jasmine Caldwell College Pamela Schiesl Mansfield Township Elementary School, Port Murray, NJ.

Annexure -1

Reading tool

1. Alphabet Level

a b c d h j l m o t r s u x b o l y f w e z n I p k n m s d w v f z e x u a

X V E Q D H Y T E X Z A P O I U Y T R E W Q L K J H G F D S A M N B V C

b d r s c o o p j I k l w v u n m h g f v v s z x q t t r r e e h f a t y r a d z

2. Word Level

CAT BAT RAT THOSE THAT THEN HERE HIS HER LIKE WHERE WE YOU ME SHE BASIC CLASS SCHOOL TEACHER APPLE MONKEY ZEBRA TRAIN BUY STUDENT PARROT FOX

Here come go learn write read active sun kite jug star noon moon book pen pencil paper board monitor

Knife onion faith black jug mug put cut but cook car care principal evening colour donkey money read write road know now jump no beat drive pen day night cricket umpire cat care cycle footpath blackboard rainbow sunflower driver doctor

3. Sentence Level

This is a cat.

It is red.

Here is a rat. It is black.

The donkeys are walking on the road.

Children are playing on the road.

It rained. **I am a boy yesterday.**

Once there was a monkey. It was very smart. It always played with the children in the street. When he saw some men, he would jump on to the tree. Its name was Dommy. Dommy was nine year old. It was very cute. Children loved it too. Dommy was a good runner also.

8

Inculcating Culture, Soft Skills and Human Values through English Language and Literature

— *Sunita Sehrawat*

The significance of English literature and language is indisputable in the present generation where the world has conglomerated into a global village. With the developing interest in the diverse cultures, literatures and technology, the importance of English is mandatory as it is the common language which connects all. When the world is becoming a melting pot it becomes equally important and the need of the hour that focus should be given on the competency of the soft skills and inculcation of human values in the students who are our future leaders. The purpose of the education is to build students who are strong in character, trustworthy, competitive, self-disciplined, loyal, and compassionate and are ready to serve humanity. Mahatma Gandhi says "Education means all-round drawing out of the best in child and man—body, mind, and spirit."

Prof B.S. Raghavan in his book "Human Values and Professional Ethics" writes "Cultivation, inculcation and fostering of human values can be said to be at the very heart of education in the best and the broadest sense of the word. In the ultimate analysis, it is not the nuts and bolts of what one learns in the class that is going to make a difference but whether the learning has been put to wise use in the service of humanity. (pg.3)

India witnessed the education system where the primary focus was on inculcation of values and building the strong character of the student. The Vedas, the Vedanta, the epics like Mahabharata and Ramayana exhibited the true values of the Indian education system.

1. Inculcating values and language skills through mythological literature

India is endowed with the rich heritage of the greatest epics in the world. The translated versions (English) of these literatures can be beneficial in multiple ways. Our education system is such that in the name of religion the absolutely essential literature which can strengthen the value system, can empower children with rich culture and simultaneously can enhance their language skills is not included in the curriculum. The Bhagavad Gita is one of the books which if included in the curriculum can help in inculcating human values along with the learning of English language. Stories from Panchatantra and the Jataka tales also serve the same purpose. A student not only gets motivated but also imbibes the values of caring, sharing and humility through these stories. The Bhagvad Gita should compulsorily be a part of education as it is the best manual to life in terms of a guide to better living psychologically, philosophically, physically and spiritually.

2. Through writing speeches and articles, conducting debates and presentations

English communication skills can be improved by introducing communication activities such as group discussions, role plays, debates, etc. in the regular curriculum. The themes of all these activities can be taken from the moral stories, the highly motivating biographies viz. biography of Abdul Kalam, Swami Dayanand Saraswati and from many other such resources. These books and activities can assist in teaching the communication skills in the best possible and easy way with the virtues of honesty and humanity in their lives. Role play activities, based on the lives and events of the great freedom fighters, leaders, and achievers in their field can be carried out. Introduction of such activities can surely enhance the language skills along with the inculcation of moral values like self-respect and respecting others, co-operation, honesty, sincerity and compassion.

There may be the chance of indiscipline and disinterestedness in the students which should be checked appropriately and some roles of negative characters may be judiciously incorporated where the immorality leads to suffering and punishment.

3. Through folktales and short stories

Murdoch (2002, p.9) explains that "short stories can, if selected and exploited appropriately, provide quality text content which will greatly enhance students' language." Short stories could be very beneficial in learning language as well as building character of a student. India has a tradition where grandparents and parents taught multiple traits through telling the stories. Including these stories and folktales in curriculum can enhance their language in a smooth fashion. Listening and reading of the short stories could offer the students great opportunities to communicate their own ideas or feelings about the issues easily.

4. Through excursion tours and trips

The 'Teaching outside the Box' theory paved the way for academic tours and trips, where students get experience of the society, culture and the environment through their own vision and develop a deeper and practical understanding of the world around them and evolve themselves in becoming better students and citizens. Such excursions help the students in learning the diverse cultures, biodiversity, and social status of different classes and still believe in the sameness of everyone. These trips also provide an opportunity for students to develop their interpersonal skills, civic management skills and organizational skills. But they should be guided well by the facilitator and should be sensitized well to the oneness of all.

During such visits, students can be asked to write reports on the places they visited, people they met and the experiences they gathered. Group discussions, speeches and articles can be asked on the same topics.

5. Evaluation

Along with the process of teaching and learning and achieving the objectives, evaluation becomes a mandatory process to check the progress of the child. Thus, testing and evaluation play a significant role in teaching and learning of any language. Language has four skills: listening, speaking, reading and writing. Taking care of these skills, different tests (oral and written) can be prepared to judge the students' skills in language. A teacher or facilitator must understand the different language acquiring skills of the students and accordingly, he judiciously must carry out the evaluation process. The diverse cultural backgrounds of the students should be kept in the mind.

According to Bloom, evaluation encompasses a broader term except examining only the academic achievements of the students. Their attitudes, personality traits, skills, character building also should be analyzed. While carrying out the evaluation process the examiner must check the presence of moral values and positive attitude of the students as we are responsible for producing the future citizens of the country. If they are only acquiring the certificates for the academics sans good attitude, probably we may lose good future leaders.

6. Rewards and punishments

Rewards and punishments have their own place and significance in the teaching learning process, however these must be used appropriately to get the desired results. While reward is a positive factor and punishment is a negative one, the teacher should be extra cautious distributing these among students, who are achievers and those who fail to achieve the objectives. Both the factors can have adverse effects, if overused. Tom Peters opines that by following the appropriate method of rewarding, excellent results can be obtained. Accordingly punishment must be appropriate to the fault and executed immediately, unbiased and result oriented, rather than punishing for the wasted efforts.

Works Cited

1. Bloom Taxonomy. http://www.nwlink.com/-donclark/hrd/bloom.html
2. Raghavan, B.S. (2009). Human Values and Professional Ethics, S. Chand & Company.
3. Murdoch, G. (2002). Exploiting well-known Short Stories for Language Skills Development. IATEFL LCS SIG Newsletter, 23, 9-17.

9

A Comparison of Elements of Language in the Works of Noam Chomsky and Panini

— *Garima Bhatnagar*

In order to understand the basis on which the multilingual aspect of the various languages in the Indian subcontinent functions, as also to trace a commonality in them, it would be interesting to see if a universal aspect of Sanskrit language can be seen through employing TGG and such means of Chomsky to Sanskrit, thereby extending it to other Indian Languages also.

Pāṇini's work became known in 19th century Europe, where it influenced modern linguistics initially through Franz Bopp, who mainly looked at Pāṇini. Subsequently, a wider body of work influenced Sanskrit scholars such as Ferdinand de Saussure, Leonard Bloomfield, and Roman Jakobson. Frits Staal discussed the impact of Indian ideas on language in Europe. After outlining the various aspects of the contact, Staal notes that the idea of formal rules in language, proposed by de Ferdinand de Saussure in 1894 and finally developed by Noam Chomsky in 1957, based on which formal rules were also introduced in computational languages, has origins in the European exposure to the formal rules of Paninian grammar.

The Chomskyan approach towards syntax, often termed generative grammar, studies grammar as a body of knowledge possessed by language users. Since the 1960s, Chomsky has maintained that much of this knowledge is innate, implying that children need only learn certain parochial features of their native languages. The innate body of linguistic knowledge is often termed Universal Grammar. From Chomsky's perspective, the strongest evidence for the existence of Universal Grammar is simply the fact that children successfully acquire their native languages in so little time. Furthermore, he argues that there is an enormous gap between the linguistic stimuli to which children are exposed and the rich linguistic knowledge they attain (the "poverty of the stimulus" argument). The knowledge of Universal Grammar would serve to bridge that gap.

His most influential and time-tested contribution to the field, is the claim that modeling knowledge of language using a formal grammar accounts for the "productivity" of language. In other words, a formal grammar of a language can explain the ability of a hearer-speaker to produce and interpret an infinite number of utterances, including novel ones, with a limited set of grammatical rules and a finite set of terms. He has always acknowledged his debt to Pāṇini for his modern notion of an explicit generative grammar although it is also related to Rationalist ideas of a priori knowledge.

Chomsky demonstrates the fact that languages are 'rule governed', and that these rules could really lead to production of language and its units. Noam Chomsky has always acknowledged his debt to Pānini for his modern notion of an explicit generative grammar. In Chomsky and Morris Halle's 1968 text *The Sound Pattern of English*, the authors give an implicit nod to the Ashtadhyayi by formulating their final rule "ā → ā", which echoes the final Pānini's final rule, "a a iti".

- Chomsky and Panini have a logical, systematic, mathematical approach to grammar.
- Both of them have garnered important and significant aspects of language and grammar from their predecessors

and have incorporated and used them to formulate their own rules, at times modifying them too.

- Both have dealt not only with the grammar but also the linguistic and finer nuances of the language.

Chomsky and Panini have tried to both shape and incorporate elements from the common language /vernacular, being spoken and written during their times. There is no classical aspect to their works as conceived by them...it is as much for the elites as it is for the poor.

Both Chomsky and Panini have taken most of the elements of language into consideration. Both have grouped the phonemes; the manner & place of their articulation viz, dental; labial, retroflex and so on. The pitch of phonemes has also been acknowledged by both of them. *However, euphonic combination, though acknowledged by Chomsky, has not been dealt separately. Similarly, there is no place for a spiritual / divine phoneme in Chomsky, whereas Panini acknowledges that.*

Both have affirmed the formation of Compound words while the order of words and their types have also been found. Morphophonemic changes are found in both Chomsky and Panini. However, Augmentation in the sense of आगम is not to be found in Chomsky. Number can be found in both Chomsky and Panini's conception of Compound words. However, evidence of assigning gender to compound words is not to be found in Chomsky's conception, present in Panini.

Noun Cases can be found by both Chomsky and Panini. However, classification of these Noun Cases according to various endings, viz., vowels, consonants, gutturals, palatals linguals, dentals, labials and so on can be found only in Panini's Grammar. Degrees of comparison, Numerals, ordinals can be found in both Chomsky's and Panini's conception of grammar. Both of them seem to admit of Tense and Mood, however, Panini can boast of having tenses 'लकार' not to be found with Chomsky. Though 'roots' have been acknowledged by Chomsky, yet there is still no parallel for the Paninian term 'धातु' and its dynamic nature. Again, though derivation and inflection are to be found in both Chomsky and Panini, but inflection from both verb and noun forms is a hallmark of Panini. Moreover, Panini's roots have been grouped in the धातुपाठ, as others in गणपाठ- However, Chomsky seems to rely only on 'lexical entries' of words. As regards Case Relations both Chomsky and Panini have laid emphasis on its significance in syntactical structure. An important point to note here is that Panini has not defined 'sentence' with as much precision as other elements. However, it still remains the most important feature of his Grammar. Relations between 'things' and 'processes', agreement of a nominal with a verb can be found in both Chomsky and Panini. However, derivational relation is a unique feature of Panini. Again linguistic representation of cases in sentence can be seen in the theories of both Chomsky and Panini. However, representation through various endings, viz, nominal verbal, suffixes and so on are found only in Panini. Other grammatical features, viz, Restrictions, Accents, Morphophonemic changes and so on are to be found in both Panini and Chomsky.

An interesting feature to note here is that Panini's emphasis regarding elements of language is more on a grouping. His conception of Ashtadhyayi is very concise and focused. One reason for this could be that he was trying to pick up elements of the vernacular language of his times and trying to reflect all possible features in his Grammar. Another reason could be that whatsoever the anthologizing act might have been, the grammatical tradition of Ancient India was primarily 'Oral' as मुखं व्याकरणम् स्मृतम्- So, the attempt at brevity and grouping could be so as to assist the fleeting human memory. A condensed grammar would definitely appeal to the masses, since it would mean 'lesser' amount to learn. At the same time, Panini was also trying to purge the language of his times by trying to maintain the standard of the language of his times by forming a rule code to be followed to the book. Thus, the traditional Paninian

Grammar has the feature of being कठस्थ. Therefore, by devising Ashtadhyayi, Panini was also trying to avoid the popular 'vulgarisms' of language prevalent in his times.

As can be clearly seen, Panini seems to be somewhat ahead of his counterpart in the sheer number of 'processes' regarding the elements of language. This clearly indicates that Chomsky's conception of Generative Grammar is rather static as compared to Panini's, who seems to be more dynamic. This is a significant point to note considering the fact that Chomsky and Panini are placed considerably far off in 'time'. Panini's Grammar and theory of language is much 'Ancient' as compared to that of Chomsky's which is more 'Modern', so to say. The only thing missing with Panini in the table is the 'Diagrammatic Representation' of his rules and processes. It is only later on, now, that reviewers / writers have started diagrammatizing Panini's work. Chomsky, however, has diagrammatical representation at the heart of his work, what with tree diagram, labeled bracket, rewrite rules and so on.

It is also interesting to note that both Panini and Chomsky have used imaginary 'symbols' for brevity and focusing on their work. For example, अण् etc, प्रत्याहार, अधिकारसूत्र अनुवृत्ति, अध्याहार and so on. Chomsky has also employed terms like 'θ', 'α', 't', $\overline{X}$ etc which seem to denote imaginary / abstract formulations.

To sum up, Panini seems to be adept at anthologizing the rules of the language of his times, which he also aimed at. However, Chomsky only seems to be putting forth Parameters and Principles. As such, the variations seen in Paninian grammar far exceed those in Chomksyan conception.

Chomsky scores over his ancient counterpart Panini, as regards to conception of a Universal Grammar.

First of all, Panini remains mute on the concept of Language Acquisition which is central to all Chomsky's concepts. Perhaps because the oral tradition was too predominant to let anyone think otherwise. Again, there is no mention of mental process in Panini's work. Whereas Chomsky conceives of grammar as reflection of mind, it may be pertinent to mention here that concepts like Language 'Acquisition' and 'Mental' or psychological processes are an evolution of the modern times. Though psychological processes were found in Panini's times, but, they were, perhaps, outside the domain of grammatical elements. There is a definite structure dependency seen in both Chomsky and Panini's grammar. Projections of lexical entries for Chomsky and those of गणपाठ and धातुपाठ can be seen for both Panini and Chomsky. Both Panini and Chomsky appear to exhibit generative functions of grammar. Language has been seen by both as a relationship between sound and meaning. Important point to note is that where Panini talks of only one language, Chomsky talks about a Universal Language, for all languages. The central part of language according to both of them is syntax, though Panini seems to involve morphophonemic changes more than others. Panini's language is definitely an E- Language, which is a physical manifestation of language. However, Chomsky finds I – Language more important as he is concerned with the speaker's knowledge (mental) of the language. Panini's Grammar seem to side with 'performance' whereas Chomsky's emphasis is on competence. Whereas, Chomsky talks of a language faculty as an important aspect of language development. Panini does not say anything about it. Both of them have structural and linguistic rules and principles. Morphophonemic changes are the most significant aspect of a language for Panini. However, for Chomsky relation between syntax and semantics is of utmost importance. Chomsky's theory relies on s – structure and d-structure, whereas Panini has no such structures. Limitations as per bounding has been acknowledged by both of them. Whereas Chomsky has a Control Theory, Panini uses techniques like अधिकारसूत्र to employ control. Roles of कारक are very important for the grammar of Panini. In contrast, there is assigning of θ-roles in the grammar of Chomsky.

Peripheral features and markedness are employed in both of them, in Panini, through *ok* and विभाषा. Whereas Chomsky's theory rests on psychological tenet of innatism, Panini doesn't say anything about it. Panini has taken into account the topical issues and objects of his times. Whereas Chomsky doesn't seem to do any such thing.

Unique aspects of Panini's Grammar

- Astadhyahi is both a theory and a grammar of Sanskrit. The theory implicit in the grammar envisages a dynamic system in which the surface variety and difference are dissolved to reveal underlying unities, wherein this has the potential to be that, wherein each has the potential to become the other.
- The special vocabularly employed as a code to denote the elements and operations of grammar. As लकार is not an actual word, but can be literally interpreted as ल.आकार, "the shape of form of *y*". A term such as अण् on the other hand, is also not an actual word and in addition, completely opaque – it is properly a symbol. The motivation for the use of such specially invented terms is economy of statement and the coded terms also represent an analysis of a particular understanding of the domain they stand for.
- The rules of Astadhyayi are "law – like generalizations the Grounds, while the संज्ञा (the categories of grammar) constitute the Reasons, or the defining vocabularly of the rules (they are all placed together in the beginning of the Grammar).
- Astadhyayi exhibits a particular "depth" of a grammatical explanation by virtue of the fact that several rules of Astadhyayi (कारक, phonological rules like that of de-aspiration, etc.) have, claimed to have, applicability to human languages in general.
- An examination of the rules and operations of Astadhyayi shows the existence of all types of grammatical explanation.

- It describes the known range of Sanskrit usage.
- Panini's grammatical description shared some of the categories of different philosophical systems such as *Vaisesika* and *Nyaya* on the one hand and, on the other influenced the development of poetics as well.
- This theory of description the fits in very well with the non-structural dimension of language, such as cognition and communication. Panini's grammar with its basic postulates of "affixation", "base", "Affix", "Deletion", "modification", "augment", inter and intra-category relations, and "hierarchy of structuration" has functioned like "a primary modeling device" and has been employed / has the potential of being employed to other symbolic systems (dance and sculpture, for example).
- Panini's Grammar is also found to exhibit generative functions of Grammar.
- Panini's grammar is also said to be appropriate for a Computer Aided Study.

Features of Chomsky's Grammar

- "A Child learning a language analyze/makes sense out of the data around him".
- As the child hears language spoken around him, he refers to his own inborn mental structure in order to make sense out of what he hears spoken.
- Existence of a modular language faculty richly endowed with innate constraints delimiting the range of NL grammars;
- Human linguistic capacities are explicable to the structure of linguistic representations, that is, the structures that the grammar of the relevant NL generates.
- The poverty of the stimulus as the key aspect of language acquisition;
- Linguistics is a subpart of theoretical psychology

- Native speakers also have the ability to relate lexical items to one another.
- One of the most remarkable features of natural languages is their property of 'efficiency'.
- The child knows the language so determined by the grammar he has acquired. The grammar is a representation of his "intrinsic competence".
- A person proceeds from a genetically determined initial state (S_0) through a sequence of states (S_1 S_2...,) finally reaching a "steady state" (S_s) which, then, seems to change only marginally
- There can be "structure – independent rule" and "structure-dependent rule".
- "Formal universals" are conditions on the form and function of the system of rules and principles that constitutes the theory of the structure of some cognitive domain.
- "Substantive Universals", which are fixed elements that enter into particular grammars.
- Phonetics, or in semantics proper, as in the intricate properties of rule ordering and application in phonology
- According to Chomsky, the subject is "exposed" to relevant information and the underlying structures are, then, "revealed" by the action of the environment.
- Universal Grammar is not learnt but already present in the mind;
- If UG is to be used fully, it will mean adapting the preceding methods or their equivalent, but that hasn't been attempted as yet.
- Much language teaching today is incompatible with a Chomskyan approach because of its Externalized-Language (E-Language) emphasis on communication and social interaction.
- Language acquisition is the interaction between specific features of the UG in the learner's mind and triggering

experience from the environment. (The NCF 2005 also states this).

- Provision of appropriate evidence, rather than communicative interaction or grammatical explanation.
- The syllabus would make use of concepts such as the pro-drop parameter or the head parameter, and the core/periphery distinction.
- L1 children start with the zero state, (S_0), and go on to steady state, (Ss). They progress from an initial state of knowing nothing, but their innate endowment to a final state of knowing everything about a particular language.
- Chomsky argues for the 'commonsense' view that only the complete knowledge of language counts, rather than intermediate states.
- The second language can also be learnt by other means than the language faculty.
- Classrooms can involve natural learning and real-life situations.
- The poverty of the stimulus argument led to the conclusion that at least some L2 learners know things they could not have acquired from the environment.
- The learners' possession of L1 is no guide in itself to languages that have other settings.
- UG is no longer available after a particular point of maturation;
- "Once some language is available, acquisition of others is relatively easy",

The study has endeavoured to compare some element of language from the works of Noam Chomsky and Panini. Though separated by a considerable gap of time, their treatment of linguistic elements and approach towards language has been much similar regarding the systematic basis and scientific inquiry. However, the two differ mainly on the fact that whereas Chomsky tries to define principles that *account for the structure and function of all languages;*

Panini is only trying to *anthologise the working of the language of his time.* The in-depth study and analysis of their works opens up a plethora of related areas to be further studied

Most of the implications of this study is regarding language development and education. Chomskyan tenets of UG can be used for L_1 and L_2 learning in educational institutions. On the other hand, Panini's precise and brief rules can be employed in language learning.

That both of them talk of general features of a language exhaustively, a general grammatical framework can be developed, as Chomsky has enunciated, for all languages. Importantly, for Indian context, tenets of both UG and Paninian grammar can be employed together to address the variations in language learning due to multilingual nature. The fact that Panini's language and methods can be seen reflected in many Indian languages as result of the linguistic evolution; and Chomsky's attempt at Universalizing Grammar; a collective approach could benefit & target the vast range of linguistic variations in India

Works Cited

Books

- Ananthanarayana, H.S., (1916). *Four Lectures on Panini's Ashtadhyayi* Annamalai University, Annamalai Nagar.
- Bhandare, V.V. (1996). *Sanskrit Speech Habits and Panini.* Mala Ahiya Takshila Hard Bounds. Malka Ganj, Delhi
- Bhandarkar, RG. (1978). *Second Book of Sanskrit.* Light and life Publishers.
- Bhat, D.N.S. (Oct. 1983) *A Critique of Chomsky's Theory of Grammar.* International School of Dravedian Linguistics. Trivandrum. India
- Burt, Marina K. (1971) *From Deep to surface structure : an introduction to transformational syntax.*
- Campbell, Lyle (2003) *The History of Linguistics.* In Aronoff, Mark & Miller, Janie Rees (ed.). *The Handbook of Linguistics.* Blackwell Publishers.
- Cardona, George (2004) *Recent Research in Paninian Studies.* Motilal Banarsidas Publishers Pvt. Ltd., Delhi
- Cook, V.J. (1989) *Chomsky's Universal Grammar. An Introduction.* Blackwell Publishers.

- Dahiya, Yajan Veer (1995). *Panini as a Linguist : Ideas and Patterns.* Eastern Book Linkers, Delhi.
- Das, Karunasindhu (1986). *Paribhasas in the Paninian System of Grammar.* Sanskrit Book Depot (P) Limited. Calcutta.
- Dikshit, Pushpa (2009). *Astadhyayi Sutrapathah of Maharsi Panini with Prakarananirdesa.* Gyanbharti Publication, Delhi. India
- Dixit, Pushpa (2009). *Ashtadhyayi Sutrapath of Maharshi Panini with Prakarananirdesa.* Gyanbharti Publication, Delhi
- Dwivedi, Dr. Kapil Dev. *Prarambhik Rachnanuvad Kaumudi.* Vishwavidyalaya Prakashan, Varanasi.
- Dwivedi, Kapildev Dr. (2009) *Praudha Rachnanuvad Kaumudi.* Vishwavidyalaya Prakashan, Varanasi.
- England, Barbara R. (1978) *Glossarized Charts of Noam Chomksy's Grammar.* Physsardt Publications, Bloomington, Indiana.
- George, Alexander (1989) *Reflections on Chomsky's* Basil Blackwell Ltd. Oxford U.K.
- Jamison, Stephanie W. (2004) Sanskrit. *In the Cambridge Encyclopedia of the World's Ancient Languages.* Cambridge University Press.
- Jigyasu, Pt. Brahdutt (ed.) (2006) *Paniniya Ashtadhyayi sutrapath.* Ramlal Kapur Trust, Rewali, Sonepat.
- Kasher, Asa ed. (1993) *The Chomskyan Turn.* Blackwell Publishers.
- Katre, S.M. (1981) *A Glossary of Grammatical Elements and Operators in Ashtadhyayi.* Central Institute of Indian Language's Manasagangotri, Mysore.
- Kiparsky, Paul. Ed. Joshi, S.D. (1979) *Panini as a Variationist.* The Poona University Press and the MIT Press.
- Kumar, Pushpendra (ed.) (August 1984) *Linguistics Thought in Ancient India.* Nag Publishers, Jawahar Nagar, Delhi-7.
- Laddu, Sureshchandra Dnyaneshwar (1974). *Evolution of the Sanskrit Language from Panini to Patanjali.* Centre of Advanced study in Sanskrit. University of Poona. Poona
- McGilvray, James ed. (2005) *The Cambridge Companion to Chomsky.* Cambridge University Press.
- Moore, Terence & Carling, Christine (1982). *Understanding Language – Towards a Post Chomskyan Linguistics.* The Macmillan Press Ltd.
- Palmarini, Massimo Piattelli (ed.) (1979) *Language and Learning – The Debate between Jean Piaget and Noam Chomsky.* Routledge & Kegan Paul London and Henley.
- Prakasam, V. (2008). *Encyclopaedia of the Linguistic Sciences. Issues and Theories.* Allied Publishers Pvt. Ltd. Delhi.

- Prakash, Satya (1984). *A Bibliography of Sanskrit Language and Literature.* Indian Documentation Service. Gurgaon.
- Richards, Jack. Platt, John, Weber, Heidi (1985). *Longman Dictionary of Applied Linguistics.* Longman Group Limited. England.
- Shastri, Chakradhar Nautiyal 'Hans' (1962) *Brihad Anuvad Chandrika.* Motilal Banarasidas, Delhi
- Shastri, Sriniwas. *Srimad Bhattoji Dixit Virarchita Sidhant Kaumudi, Karakaprakaranam.* Sahitya Bhandar, Subhash Bazar, Meerut.
- Sreedharan, M.S., (2005) *Bhartiya Vigyan Manjusha Treasure Trove of Ancient Indian Sciences.* Publications Division, Ministry of Information and Broadcasting, Govt. of India.
- Staal, J.F. (1967). *Word Order in Sanskrit and Universal Grammar.* D. Reidel Publishing Company Dordrecht – Holland.
- Stam, James H. (1976) *Inquiries into the origin of language, the fate of question.* Harper & Row, Publishers.
- Vyomshekhar, Bishan Lal Gaur Dr. (1985) *Paniniya Ashtadhyayi Ke Rachanasidhant.* Lokalok Prakashan, Ghaziabad.

Journals

- Ananthanarayana, H.S. (Jan – June 1970). The Karaka Theory and Case Grammar. *Indian Linguistics.* Vol. 31, No. 1 – 2.
- Croft, William and Poole, Keith T. (2008) Inferring Universals from grammatical variation: Multidimensional scaling for typological analysis. *Theoritical Linguistics.* Vol. 34- 1.Berlin – Network.
- Deshpande M. Madhav (Mar – Dec 1981) Revisiting Panini 7.3.73. *Indian Linguistics* Vol. 42 No. 1
- Joshi, Laxman Venkatesh (1965) Panini and the Paniniyas on Samhita. *Indian Linguistics.* Vol. 26.
- Subrahmanyam, P.S.(1985) Panini and Semantically Deviant Sentences. *Indian Linguistics,* Vol. 46, No. 1
- Ranade, H.G. (1974) Parts of speech in Sanskrit. *Indian Linguistics.* 35. 129 – 38.

Table 1: Phonological, Morphological and Syntactical Elements of Language.

S. No.	*Element*	*Panini*	*Chomsky*
1.	PHONETICS /PHONOLOGY		
	(a) Brevity	✓	✓
	(b) Grouping of phonemes	✓	✓

	(c) Placement of phonemes	✓	✓
	(d) Spiritual/ Divine	✓	✗
	(e) Elision	✓	✓
	(f) intervention	✓	✓
	(g) Dental (dentolabial)	✓	✓
	Labial	✓	✓
	Retroflex	✓	✓
	(h) Consonants	✓	✓
	Length	✓	✓
	(i) Pitch	✓	✓
	Acute	✓	✓
	Grave	✓	✓
	Circumflex	✓	✓
	(j) Euphonic Combination	✓	✗
	Vowel-Vowel	✓	✗
	Consonant- Vowel	✓	✗
	Consonant- Consonant	✓	✗
2.	MORPHOLOGY		
	A.(a) Compound Words	✓	✓
	Adverbial	✓	✓
	Determinative	✓	✓
	Possessive	✓	✓
	Co-ordinative	✓	✓
	(b) Order (words or phrases in a compound word)	✓	✓
	Elision or non elision	✓	✓
	(c) Morpho-phonemic changes	✓	✓
	Augmentation	✓	✗
	Substitution	✓	✓
	(d) Number in Compound Words	✓	✓
	(e) Gender in Compound Words	✓	✗
	B NOUNS (Cases)	✓	✓
	(a) Nouns ending in		
	Vowels	✓	☒
	Consonants	✓	✗
	Gutturals	✓	✗

	Palatals	✓	✗
	Linguals	✓	✗
	Dentals	✓	✗
	Labials	✓	✗
	Nasals	✓	✗
	Semi- vowels	✓	✓
	(b) Degrees of Comparison	✓	✓
	(c) Numerals	✓	✓
	(d) Ordinals	✓	✓
	C. Pronouns	✓	✓
	Personal	✓	✓
	Demonstrative	✓	✓
	Relative	✓	✓
	Interrogative	✓	✓
	Honorific	✓	✓
	Pronomial	✓	✓
	D. Tense (and Mood)	✓	✓
	E. Roots/ Conjugation	✓	✓
	(a) Voices	✓	✓
	Derivation	✓	✓
	Inflection	✓	✓
	(b) Grouping of Roots	✓	✗
	(c) Tenses	✓	✓
	F . Suffix	✓	✓
	(a) Primary Suffixation-Categories/ Processes	✓	✓
	(b)Secondary Suffixation	✓	✓
3.	SYNTAX	✓	✓
	(a) Case Relation Locative	✓	✓
	Dative	✓	✓
	Nominative	✓	✓
	Accusative	✓	✓
	Genitive	✓	✓
	(b) Relation between things and 'processes'	✓	✓

	(c) Co-referential elements in Speech	✓	✓
	(d) Derivational Relation among sentences	✓	✗
	(e) Association of a nominal verb with a verb	✓	✓
	(f) Linguistic Representatoin of Cases in sentences	✓	✓
	Representation by	✓	✓
	Nominal Endings	✓	✗
	Verbal Endings	✓	✗
	Primary Suffixes	✓	✗
	Secondary Suffixes	✓	✗
	Compound Formation	✓	✓
	(h) Nominalisation	✓	✓
	(i) Verbalisation	✓	✓
	(j) Grammatical features	✓	✓
	Morphophonemic Changes	✓	✓
	Placement of Accents	✓	✓
	Selection of Derivative Suffixes	✓	✓
	Selection of Verbal Endings	✓	✓
	Restriction on Compound Formation.	✓	✓

Table 2: Elements (Concepts of Language in Grammar of Noam Chomsky and Panini)

Sl. No.	*Element*	*Panini*	*Chomsky*
1.	Language Acquisition	Does not mention	Yes
2.	Mental Processes	Does not mention	Language related to mind
3.	Structure Dependency	Is Present	Is Present
4.	I-Language/ E-Language	E-Language	I-Language
5.	Projection	Is Present	Is Present
6.	Generative Function	Exhibits	Exhibits
7.	Relationship between Sound and Meaning	Establishes such relationship	Establishes such relationship
8.	Lexical Entries	Ancillary text, dhatupath, ganapath etc.	Reliance on lexical entries
9.	Central Area of Language	Syntax	Syntax
10.	Performance/Competence	performance	competence

11.	Language Faculty	Does not mention	Establishes language faculty
12.	Rules and Principles	Establish and follow	Establish and follow
13.	Significant aspect of language	Morphophonemic changes	Syntax and Phonology
14.	Deep Structure and Surface Structure	No d-structure, s-structure	Significance of d-structure and s-structure
15.	Bounding	Limitations thorugh Bounding	Limitations through bounding
16.	Control	Adhikaar Sutra	Control Theory
17.	Case Roles	Roles of Karak	Theta Roles
18.	Core & Periphery	Shown through 'va', 'vibhasha'	Core & Periphery established
19.	Markedness	Departures allowed to assimilate	Markedness established
20.	Innatism	Does not mention	Basis of Linguistic Theory
21.	Topical Issues / Objects	Mentioned in Ashtadhyayi	No Mention

10

Plurality of Resources in English Language Teaching and Learning in Rural Areas

— *Malvika Oberoi*

Language is our primary source of communication. It is the method through which we share our ideas and thoughts with others. The study of English language in this age of globalization is essential. It has become the most important language of communication in different countries. In India, people of different states have their own languages. English language has come to us as a connecting link among various states in India. During the British rule, English was the medium of teaching both at school and college level. When Britishers became traders, they opened many institutions and the demand of English was raised in India. Social Reformers like Raja Rammohan Roy was in favor of English education. After Macaulay Minutes, English became a popular medium of instruction in India.

United Nations has recognized five languages as its official languages and, English takes the first position because of its background, international acclaim of easy access to the people. English has emerged as the most important global language. This language has helped different countries to come and work together as it is also the language of trade. In the other words, it has helped in improving the International Relations. It is a wrong view to hold that it is a language of the British alone, English has evolved to be a language of science and technology. Majority of all important books for higher studies are written in English. Apart from all these, we have sufficient ground for supporting the use of English for commercial and economic purposes in our country.

It is the responsibility of every individual to work hard to acquire good communication skills. In India, there is a great difference of language which is observed in the lives of rural and urban children. Urban children get more opportunities in learning English as compared to rural children. They get special training at school level in order to acquire skills of reading, writing, listening and speaking. Each subject is taught in the medium of English. There is an utmost demand of English speaking teachers. Looking at all these areas, it is evident that rural students lack these skills and have limited exposure to learn English.

Having a good hold at any language requires a lot of practice. This paper deals with providing innovative and effective techniques in English teaching to rural children. Today, modern techniques have replaced the traditional practices. Teaching has become much easier with the role of media. Teaching English with this new technology has produced a positive attitude among the children and their willingness to learn the target language.

Lifestyle of Rural and Urban children

Urban children have privilege of learning English through advanced techniques than rural children. In rural areas, the primary aim of teaching is to pass the exam. Bookish knowledge is only received by the children. Translation of content from English to Hindi is widely seen. Even after studying in school for so many years, students hesitate to speak English. It is the moral responsibility of the teacher in rural areas to motivate children regarding the importance of English language. They should have an honest approach while dealing with the children. The focus should be on the availability of the resources for learning a new language.

The flow of technology from urban areas to rural areas can help in the development of rural areas. Internet is a basic medium through which any person can attain knowledge but it requires a good understanding in English to access Internet. Every material available online is in English, so to process the information, learning English is compulsory. Therefore, we can't deny the fact that English is the most important element in the process of communication. More job opportunities are in the hand of those who are well versed in English. Hence, it can help in the development of the rural areas which can further lead to the development of the country.

Why rural children are lagging behind?

It is a very known fact that India is a densely populated country and illiteracy rate is also high. This is especially seen in the rural parts of India. The very first factor that hinders the growth of these children is illiteracy in their families. Lack of guidance from the parents is observed. Lack of awareness is the root cause. In addition to this, financial burden and socio-economic conditions are also a cause of this. On the other hand, urban children get many privileges.

If rural children are well versed in English, they can get better employment opportunities. The reasons they lag behind are as follows:

1. **Financial Burden:** The standard of living of rural people is not high. So, they can't afford to send their children to prestigious schools and colleges. Lack of guidance from their parent's side is also an issue. Incentives should be provided to these children for their better future. Also, providing them with the scholarships can boost their growth. Quality of books and new sources of learning should be promoted. There should be awareness regarding the schemes that the government provides to the rural sections of the society.

In order to ease the financial burden, special funds should be generated.

2. **Infrastructural issues:** Lack of infrastructure hinders quality education in India both at primary and secondary level. Living in Twenty First Century, India still faces the problem of poor infrastructure. A good library with quality books, smart boards and internet facility should be mandatory in the school for yielding better results.
3. **Transportation costs:** Travelling from rural areas to urban areas is a time taking process. The transport facility is still not developed in some areas. Hence, it is a cause of concern for the students because it disturbs the regularity of classroom teaching. If the transport facility is well developed, it can increase the enrollment rate of students in the school. In many cases, it is seen that roads are not constructed properly. So, proper maintenance of roads is required to upgrade the transport system.
4. **Shortage of teaching faculty:** There are many posts that are vacant. So, very few teachers are overburdened with the work. This decreases the efficiency of teachers as they are not able to plan their lectures properly.To have quality teaching in schools, a teacher should get ample time for the preparation and implementation of lectures. The other thing that bothers is the shortage of number of teachers in the school. Most of the teachers prefer to teach urban students rather than teaching rural children. They sometimes switch their jobs. This mindset leads to the inadequate teaching staff in the school. Motivation should not only be given to the students but to the teachers as well.
5. **Right methodology is lacking:** English is not the mother tongue of Indian students.We learn English as a second language or as a target language. If a right technique is not implemented, it creates problems in the learning process. A teacher has to adopt various methods to teach English.One

of the following methods is Translation Method which is a best suitable method to learn a second language but it weakens the creativity of students. Direct method can be taught with the translation method. It is advisable for the students to take part in group discussions because it will help them in achieving the desirable results.

Role of English Language at School level

Focus should also be given on four skills namely Listening, Speaking, Reading and Writing.

(1) **Listening**- It comes first in the order as no language could be learnt without listening to it. Even a new born is capable of speaking a particular language after listening to it for many months. Our syllabus emphasises more on writing and reading of English language. Lack of speaking skills mean, not having a proper guidance in listening skills.

Provisions of audio visual aids should be given at the school level.

To be done-

- A special listening skills class should be organized by the school once or twice a week. It should contain recorded speeches and discussions on recent topics. It can enrich the listening skills as well as make students aware about the ongoing issues.
- English movie session could also be introduced which can fulfill the purpose of both learning and entertainment.
- Listening to the speeches of famous politicians and persons can help them motivate to plan their future and can instill the values among the students.
- Watching English news headlines can also benefit the children for their overall development apart from just gaining bookish knowledge.

The above activities can help students to improve their vocabulary and pronunciations to have a good hold on the language.

(2) **Speaking**: Speaking exercises should be designed in such a way that students get friendly environment so that they can cope up with their problem of hesitation. This can be improved through practices such as -

- Teaching them day to day expressions of greeting someone, self introduction, apologies, complementing someone, formal and informal sentences, words and many others.
- Role play is an important learning based exercise which can also be imparted in schools as well as colleges.

(3) **Reading**: Student's linguistic skills can be improved through reading exercises. We can enhance these skills by following such practices-

- In the starting stage, students should be asked to read aloud. It is done so in order to correct their mistakes in pronunciation. These exercises can be done in the classrooms which can boost the confidence among the students.
- Assignments of reading should be made in such a way that it contains proper pause and stress.
- It can help in enhancing the vocabulary of the students. If students are stuck with any difficult word, allow them to guess the word instead of spoon feeding them.

(4) **Writing**: This skill can be improved in the following ways-

- Memory retention games can be introduced in the classroom. It can help in improving the concentration as well as impart the fun element among the students.
- Jotting down the news headlines in their own language. This task can be given to the students on daily basis.
- Other activities like writing short articles, diary and article writing can also be added to boost the writing skills.

The above activities if done in a proper way can help in increasing the output by yielding better results. There are high chances of committing errors by the students but with patience and encouragement, a teacher can become a good guide. Also, true learning can never take place without committing errors. In all the exercises, the role of a teacher comes into play. It is the duty of the teacher to create a friendly environment in the classroom in which students can easily interact and exercise their tasks fearlessly.

Apart from the above practices, the following exercises should also be adopted in the English language class:

- **Group Discussions**: This exercise can be arranged in the classrooms. Students can be given any topic according to their taste. If the topic is somehow unfamiliar to them, teacher should explain the meaning in the class so that students could go ahead with the discussion. Every student should get a chance to speak. This will help students attain confidence and master the speaking skills.
- **Reading out loud**: Students should read texts loudly in the class. Teachers should listen to them carefully and check their pronunciation. This exercise will help students to overcome their fear of speaking.
- **Role play**: To make language learning interesting, role plays can be organized in the classrooms. Every student should get a chance to play some role or the other. Learners should play their part naturally with a touch of expressions.

Role of English language at College level

English plays an important role at college level-

- In India, Universities and colleges use English as a medium of instruction.

  To get admission into any degree program in any educational institution or foreign universities, English is the most important language as interviews and group discussions are conducted through this medium only before the selection process.

- Knowing English is a pre condition before getting any ordinary job in India as well. The ones having good communication skills can get a job easily.
- In this era of Globalization, exchange of ideas happens in English language.

Role of teachers at College level

College education is at great demand nowadays. It is the moral responsibility of English language teachers to teach English in an effective way at the college level.

- The class has amalgamation of different groups of people based on their economic and social status. It is the duty of the teacher to get along with every student of the class.
- Special attention should be given to the students who belong to regional background.
- The institutions should organize extra classes in English for weak students. Also, a diploma course can be arranged in the college premises to make children develop fluency.
- Students should be motivated regularly. Teachers should guide them properly about the upcoming job opportunities.
- Proper evaluation should be done in the organization. Separate exams should be conducted that will check all the skills- Reading, writing, speaking and listening.
- Lastly, results should be given in a proper manner. Children should know about their mistakes and correct answers. This will help achieve the specific target.

  All the above mentioned things will help a child to overcome the fear of English and it can mould the overall personality of the child.

Problems faced by the teachers at College level

- The overcrowded class affects quality teaching. Teachers are not able to pay proper attention to the students because of the increase in class size.

- Attending classroom without textbooks is an increasing trend which we see nowadays.
- Lack of attendance in the classrooms tests affects the quality of teaching. Teachers can't properly examine the students and it further leads to the discouragement of sincere students as well as teachers.
- Shortage of teaching staff and proper facilities disturbs the classroom teaching.
- Language barrier is also a problem. Students using their regional language in the classroom affects the entire class.
- Literature oriented syllabus is dominant which does not help in the overall development of the students. Language oriented syllabus should be introduced to help them become good communicators and achieve fluency.

Things to be avoided

The above problems are present everywhere at the university level but there are certain things that can be avoided by the teacher which are as follows:

- Try to make teaching more interesting. Traditional methods of teaching can make children feel less motivated. Innovative practices can enhance learning process which can further lead to better results.
- Teachers should feel contented while teaching. They should not think of this profession as a burden.
- Some teachers do not plan their lectures properly. It is advised to set a plan before going to the class. They should make a monthly or weekly plan while teaching.

Teachers should be committed towards their profession. They should adopt advanced level teaching methodologies and have a friendly atmosphere in the classroom. They should motivate their children in such a way that their students not only use English language in the classroom but outside the classroom as well. This will help children to learn English faster in an effective way. It is a well known fact that the journey of every student is different. The learning speed of every learner differs from one another. It is the duty of the teacher to formulate their strategies in such a ways that it helps learners to face competition and challenges.

Way Forward

It is very important to learn and teach English in an effective manner. Finding new and innovative ways to teach English to rural students is required. A teacher should emphasis on designing their own teaching material. It will help in making language learning simple and easy. Encourage the shy learners to come forward and involve them in various tasks. A teacher should pay attention to the interests of every student by motivating him/her to achieve higher goals in life. In a diversified class, teacher should help all the learners to respect diversity .Syllabus should be taught in such a way that it fulfills the requirement of the children and they could stand parallel to those of urban students. It is the sole responsibility of a teacher to make their students more competitive. Though, the rural students have immense potential to achieve great opportunities in life but they lag behind because of some issues.

The standard of English teaching is not at its full potential in rural India. If proper guidance is given to these students, they can definitely learn English in a better manner. Learning a second language does not mean that we should neglect out mother tongue. It is as important as learning a new language.

Textbooks should also be written in an interesting manner. It is widely seen that only urban life is highlighted rather than rural life. This practice should be curbed. If rural students are given quality education, they can stand on equal platform with the urban students. This will also help in getting rid of the sense of insecurity in them. It will also help in achieving the dream of rural youth.

If proper training is given, students will be able to get their desired jobs and can perform well in their professional life.

Conclusion

It is clear that changes are required in the rural areas regarding the education system. There are many children who do not get the benefits of the schemes that are sponsored by the government. Teaching rural children has become a necessity to have a better and secured future. Thus, the primary role of a teacher is to find effective strategies to make teaching interesting. A good interaction among the teachers and students is required in order to build confidence of students. Teachers should have a healthy relationship with the students which can lead to the overall development of the students.

They should also shape the minds of the students so that they can face the modern day challenges. Creativity should be enhanced in the schools to make teaching interesting. English teachers who teach especially in the rural areas need to have patience. They are asked to show excellent results in such adverse conditions. Putting less strain among children can give a boost to literacy rates in the country. Thus, we can make India a powerful country by eradicating illiteracy from India. It is also important to bridge the gap between urban and rural areas.

Works Cited

Alam, Q.Z. (1995). *English Language Teaching in.* New Delhi: Atlantic Publishers and Distributers.

Barley, Z., & Brigham, N. (2005). *Preparing Teachers to Teach in Rural Schools.* United States: The Ball State University.

Betageri, G. (2013). Impact of English Language Teaching on the Communication Skills of Rural Students. *International Journal on English Language and Literature.*

Kelly, A.V. (1978). *Mixed Ability Grouping.* London: Harper & Row Publishers.

Panchal, M. R. (1984). *Teaching of English.* New Delhi: Vikas Publishing House Pvt. Ltd.

Saraswathi, N. (2003). *Communicative Competence in English.* New Delhi: Discovery Publishing House.

Vandrik, S. (2014). The role of social class in English language education. *Journal of Language, Identity and Education.*

Url, P. (1996). *A Course in Language Teaching: Theory and Practice.* Great Britain: Cambridge University Press.

11

Shifting from Quantitative Assessment to Qualitative Assessment of English Language Skills in India

— *Nidhi Pradeep Sharma*

Introduction

English as one of the global language has acquired higher importance over a period of time in India, reason being its promotion by native English speakers during the colonial rule. Subsequently, dominance of English in Information Communication Technology and globalization has further contributed in making it a global language. Today, the knowledge of English is not just an essential skill but a basic competency which can be a tool for empowering people and nation. A perceived fear of hegemony of English on vernacular language may make people reluctant in accepting the fact that English is an integral part of our language skills in the present time but it cannot be denied that it has become a necessary skill today. It has gained immense significance in India due to increasing stature of India in global economy. India being one of largest country in terms of population and one of the largest economies by Purchasing Power Parity (PPP), the need for skilled manpower in India is quite obvious and growing. English Language skills can help India to achieve its objective to further develop its economy through trade relationship with western world or other countries where business language is primarily English. This makes requirement of Standard English in India even more pertinent. Ignoring this fact is likely to affect the prospective of the country adversely. Additionally, English is also used for official purposes by the government of India along with Hindi. English as an official language is widely used in national, political, commercial, educational and cultural communication in India but India still needs to catch up in terms of proficiency with the rest of the world.

Teaching and learning of English language skills in India especially in schools and colleges lacks a unified approach and there are diverse methods followed which keeps outcomes of learning scattered. The objectives of outcome are more achievement oriented than proficiency oriented and assessments are mostly objective in nature in terms of marks or grade which fails to measure a person's skills qualitatively. There is need to rethink on the objectives of learning, teaching and assessment of English language skills in order to define the measurable outcomes rather subjectively. It is important to outline what learners need to learn, what parameter of knowledge and skills are required to achieve the objectives of learning so that a language can be effectively used for communication and on that basis outcomes parameters of assessment must be determined which would ease teaching and learning approaches, processes and modalities for all components of language viz. listening, speaking, reading and writing. This would leave fair scopes for innovations in English language teaching, learning in schools and colleges in India. In order to address this requirement of a modern day learner, current evaluation pattern must be discussed and suggestive approach towards assessment of English language skills should be thought of.

Quantitative approach towards learning

National curriculum framework 2005 released by NCERT perceives English language a threat to native languages. It outlines the objective that English be treated as a subject rather than a skill building means. However, a position paper by National Focus Group on Teaching of English released by National Council of Educational Research and Training (NCERT) in 2006 discusses in its executive summary broadly and not limited to English language only, two fold aims of a language curriculum where in first aim is to attain basic proficiency in any language as in natural language and secondly it views language as an instrument in developing abstract thoughts and acquiring knowledge in an individual. The paper also discusses the need for revision in evaluation practices in schools. It raises concern about English language being the prime reason for failure of students at 10 grade level. It also points out that "Language evaluation need not be tied to achievement with respect to particular syllabi, but must be reoriented to the measurement of language proficiency"(p.5). There is need to develop such evaluation system wherein finer proficiencies of skills of language would be measured rather than overall grade or score based on achievement oriented testing.

Students, especially, at the college level manage to pass examination but they are not well versed with practical utilization of English language skills. Main aim of learning any language is to be able to practically use it for communication in real life situations but unfortunately there is only development of reading and writing skills of English language that also inadequately or rather say passively in our current English language teaching and learning system, speaking and listening skills are almost neglected. Consequently, a person at graduate or a post graduate level is not able to write or speak proper English. Language skills, specifically English language skills are inefficiently developed in a learner even at the stage of higher education and this is because our system through which they pass fails to cater their needs at every stage of learning.

Moving towards Qualitative Approach of learning

Generally speaking, living in society, a person needs to communicate in specific environment, circumstances and particular field and for that action oriented approach towards language learning is needed. From primary learning to adult learning, language learning is a life-long process. So, it is important to define objectives at the different stages of language learning (primary, secondary and higher) for harmonious growth of language skills in a person. Relationship between needs, objectives, context and methods of teaching and learning and assessment of learning outcomes must be concordant.

Objectives of assessment should be in coherence with the needs of learners and must be transparent enough and it should assess linguistic skills subjectively and not objectively. Both teachers and learners must be aware of their own progress of language skills rather than objectively performing on a certain external benchmarks of evaluations. There must be a democratic approach towards language learning focusing on actual requirements of learners. Communicative activities, strategies and competence must be accurately described at each stage, and benchmarks of achieving these competencies must be set at different levels of learning (primary, secondary and higher). There should be a clear successive road map for each higher stage of skills development. This would determine what is already learnt and what is yet to be learnt, in order to achieve desired level of learning at different stages. Learning as an ongoing process which must include self evaluation and the aim of evaluation must be to enable learners to analyse their communicative competencies and step by step growth through self awareness. So, to achieve this purpose of learning, there is a need to reshape the outcome parameters and nature of assessment at the different stages of learning which would be based on qualitative approach.

There are four sub-skill sets that form comprehensive language proficiency viz. listening, reading, speaking and writing and have four major activities involved in it like reception, production, interaction and mediation. Achievements of learners must be evaluated on the basis of me measuring positive outcome proficiency of these skills, rather than pointing out negative deficiencies of a person's language competence, for instance while evaluating an essay it would be better to focus on the impacts of mistakes on written communication rather than focusing on numbers or quantities of mistakes. This will be focusing on positive communication rather than negative aspects of the writer's writing which would assist in improving the quality of language skill. Speaking ability of a person could be tested by pointing out the errors linguistically while focusing on how a person is able to pass the message to other person and communicate well. Listening ability should be tested on the basis of how well a person understands main ideas, special factual information and recognizes opinions, attitudes and purpose of a speaker. Similarly, a wide range of reading skills can be assessed including reading for gist, reading for main ideas, reading for details, understanding inferences and implied meaning and recognizing writer's opinions and attitudes by developing reading skills like skimming, scanning and extensive reading. Reading must test how efficiently a person is able to comprehend a text. Receptive and expressive vocabulary can also be developed in the same way which would contribute in improving quality of language skills. This qualitative approach towards assessment may help a learner to analyse where one stands in present state of knowledge of a language and would contribute in making worthwhile objectives of assessments which would be communication oriented. Levels of these qualitative assessments may vary at different stages of learning and should be age appropriate, from a basic learner to higher level learner.

Test as the biggest impediment in language learning

For most learners, assessment is a source of stress which does not motivate further learning. Assessment design in our education has always been recalling based which tests more of retention capacity rather than testing the learning development. Open book tests are hardly experimented in our system of language learning. The pressure of memorising is definitely on the learner as they have the pressure of scoring in the exams from family and peers as well.

Use of technology in assessment

Having one or two assessment in a year does not help the learning, especially in learning a language. As we have moved a great deal in the era where frequent self-assessment is possible, technological solutions can be applied so that frequent assessment can happen. This will speed up the process of learning. Assessment for various features of grammar, lexis, speech, qualitative writing, and pronunciation, reading skills through unseen texts, listening for implied meaning, listening for information or gist is now possible through software applications. This would eliminate the burden on a learner to memorise mechanically the things for clearing the exam. Instead, assessment should be designed in a way that their skill levels are targeted in the progressive stages of schooling without the burden of qualifying marks.

Separation of literary learning from skill based learning

Promotion of cultural literature should be there in the syllabus so that literary work is introduced to the learner if they wish to enter in literary field like other specialised studies such as science, social sciences and mathematics which are introduced to students in secondary education so that their interest can stem out. However, it would be prudent approach to separate literary learning from the communicative skills based learning for better outcome.

There is a strong need to divide language learning into two parts, literature based learning and communicative skills based learning. This is necessary because skill based learning has certainly precedence over literary learning due to the modern day requirements. There is no need to ignore either but they should be learnt as two distinct linguistic entities. Once this is done, skill based learning needs to be broken down into 4 levels of language skills acquisition for each of the sub skills sets viz. reading, listening (receptive skills), writing and speaking (production).

Assessment Parameters

There is a need to have clear transition in four levels from basic to elementary, to intermediate and then to advanced. This should be achieved in four phases of learning viz. basic at primary schooling stage; elementary at secondary schooling stage; intermediate at higher secondary schools and advanced at senior at tertiary level.

However, there is an important point to consider that in our education system, we have different categories of schools viz. elite schools, private schools, schools managed by trusts and government schools run by municipal or local bodies. These schools have different levels of inputs in terms of resource for learning and availability of trained teachers. Thinking from larger perspective, it is pertinent to focus on government and trust based schools, where skills are most deficient. Students of English medium schools are anyway able to manage skills where they learn most subjects through English instructions. To bring the government or semi-government schools at par with English medium schools would need a fresh approach. Following fundamental (not fully elaborated) qualitative assessment benchmark at different levels of education is likely to solve the issue.

(a) **Basic level benchmark for assessment with reception and production:** At basic level achievement, learner is able to read very simple text and understand simple familiar expressions relevant from daily life like introduction, sharing personal details including ability to ask or answer questions related to immediate need, ability to ask question or answer questions pertaining to family, routine, likes & dislikes, and activities. This is possible when the communication is consciously made at the learner's pace of receiving and transmitting communication.

(b) **Elementary level benchmark for assessment with reception and production:** At this level of achievement, learner is able to read simple text without efforts and translate the text with mixed success. Achievement of this level means learner is able to describe things like events, incidences, occurrences, things of interests with mixed success in terms of linguistic quality of production (speaking and writing).

(c) **Intermediate level benchmark for assessment with reception and production:** Achievement of this level by the learner would mean that a learner is able to read complex text without efforts and understand fully the complex abstract ideas in the text. Attainment of this level means a person can easily describe things, like events, incidences, occurrences, things of interests vividly and accurately in terms of linguistic quality of production. At this level learner is also able to express abstract ideas like expressing views, opinions, and speculation fluently.

(d) **Advanced Level benchmark for assessment with reception and production:** Reaching at this level, one can receive complex to very complex ideas in text at greater speed and can also reproduce or respond it with ease. At this level, lexis and grammatical range is quite high to understand and express abstract ideas with greater ease. The production i.e. oral communication and written communication is without any noticeable efforts. At this level, one can respond spontaneously without any search for expression and one has good control on the language with fewer mistakes.

Need for a clear description of the assessment for devising the curriculum

It is high time to define what exactly we expect learners to achieve without too much focussing on examination outcome. Innovation should have a greater great place for learning. How a person wants to achieve, should also not be enforced. Freedom to learn in class-room or out of classroom should be encouraged but learners should know what and when to achieve. If there is a clear policy of desired outcome, it would be easy to standardise English learning and teaching in schools and colleges. The present state of affair is definitely going to improve in the time to come. There is a need to devise a language assessment framework to meet our national, cultural and social objectives.

Conclusion

To sum up, it can be said that instead of merely focusing on structures and grammatical accuracy, language testing must focus on how a person can use a language in real time situation for practical communication. For making these changes actually possible in assessment of language skills, it would not be sufficient to only remodel our assessment system, but approach to other learning variables like teaching, learning and curriculum also needs to be revisited. Teachers and curriculum, two major variables of learning have to be made efficient by keeping in mind the objectives of learning, then only this type of qualitative assessment would be effective enough to reach its goal. Once, we have a well-organized language framework, pedagogical work would become easier, leaving great room for innovation in language learning.

Works Cited

Council of Europe: Modern Language Division. *Common European Framework of References for Languages: Teaching, Learning and Assessment (CEFR).* Cambridge University Press, 2001.pdf

Dr Behera, Arun. "Elt in India: An Analysis". *International Journal on studies in English Language and Literature (IJSELL),* Vol.1, no.1, March 2013,P: 1-5,www.arcjournals.org, © ARC Journal. pdf

K.V.B. Ravindra Babu and Prof. K. Ratna Shiela Mani. "Where do We Stand on CEFR? An Analytical Study on ESL Learners' Language Proficiency". *Language in India: India's Higher Education Authority UGC Approved List of Journals,* Vol.18, 12 December 2018, www.languageinindia.com, ISSN 1930-2940.pdf

Little, David. "State of the art article: *The Common European Framework of Reference for Languages*: Content, Purpose, Origin, Reception and Impact". *Cambridge journals*, 2006, doi :10.1017/S0261444806003557.pdf

National Curriculum Frame work. New Delhi: National Council of Educational Research and Training, 2005.Pdf

Teaching of English: Position Paper, National Focus Group. 1st.,ed New Delhi: National council of Educational Research and Training, March 2006.pdf

12

Strategies for Teaching First Generation Learners Knock-Knock, Listen to Me

—*Arti Qanungo*

Introduction

Listening skill development means that the competency to understand and comprehend whatever has been said in the listening activity. It has been observed that even after many years of English teaching, the students are not able to comprehend what they listen. There are several reasons for this. Here, I am specifically dealing with the First Generation Learners.

First Generation Learner – refers to the students who are the first one in their entire generation to go to school and receive an education or whose parents have attended the formal education system up to primary levels of schooling. Here it is further specified that the parents have not studied English language. In such situations, the students do not feel comfortable with the language. English language is an alien language for them and they try to escape from it.

In this paper, I would first address the importance of making students comfortable with the language and remove their hesitation. To combat the unwillingness of the students in learning the language, it is very important to sensitize the students about the need and importance of the language in their life. This helps in motivating the students in connecting themselves with the language.

Strategies for teaching English to the First Generation Learners- Most of the students are children of housemaids, hawkers, vegetable sellers, rickshawwalas, etc. They are unfamiliar with the words and vocabulary of English language. They hesitate in listening to the language. Moreover the focus is only on reading and writing so that the students only read the question and write the answer in order to pass the examination. The listening part of the language is the most neglected part in English language teaching.

This paper is concerned with the need to improve the listening skills in the government school students. Most of the teachers have faced the challenge of developing listening skills in English language among the students. English is the second language in India. Listening is the fundamental skill in language acquisition. It is an important SKILL because this is how we naturally learn a language.

A child learns a language by listening. If we want a Child to Speak in English we should provide ample opportunities of listening.

Knock-Knock, listen to me is an innovative strategy which is the need of the hour. I ask my students to listen to the audio with their eyes shut, so that only their auditory senses guide them and help them pick up the correct enunciation and natural flow of language.

Every child is different, every child is unique. So the teaching strategies for First Generation Learners is a wide array of simple and feasible methods suited to their needs . when the students feel the need of English language in their daily lives, it empowers them.

Purpose of the Study

The purpose of this paper is to design strategies for First Generation Learners, so that they are able to comprehend the information after listening to the content in English language.

1. The students are able to feel comfortable with English language.
2. The students are willing to learn the language and remove their hesitation.
3. The students are able to develop Listening Skills.

Research Question

The hesitant and uncomfortable students, who are the first generation learners felt embarrassed when they are unable to communicate in English. They lack confidence. To deal with this challenge, I need to answer the following questions

(a) How to make my students feel comfortable?

(b) How to combat the unwillingness of my students to learn?

(c) What strategies should be adopted to teach First Generation Learner?

How to Teach English Language to First Generation Learners

For developing the listening skills,

"Just Develop A Habit."

=> There is no need to spend extra money

=> There is no need to waste time.

=> There is no need of any extra material.

Just utilize, what is available."

In government schools, there are many constraints. Instead of crying for those problems, we can effectively utilize what is available to us.

First Activity in My Class

- Instruct the students to close their eyes.
- Select one student and take her out of the classroom.
- The student says Hello from outside the class.

- The rest of the students will listen to the voice and then tell the name of the child.
- This activity will be done with every student.

The students enjoyed this activity very much and listened to the voice of their fellow classmates attentively. They felt comfortable in the class.

Second Activity in My Class

I instruct the students to listen carefully and follow my instructions.

- Show me your little finger of your left hand.
- Then I will say something and do something else. For example, I will (visually) touch my chin and (verbally) direct students to touch their cheeks.

My Observation

Almost every student touched their chin instead of the cheeks. All the students laughed and enjoyed the activity very much.

Third Day of My Activity

The students told me that they performed the activity on Day 2 at home also with their siblings and parents. This shows that the students are now taking interest in the Listening activities.

It is imperative for the teacher to be creative in making the classroom environment joyful and adapting it according to the needs of the students.This is done by sensitizing the students for the listening activity that involves everybody .

I spoke 3 or 4 simple sentences in English .

(Pre-Requisite : Instruct the students to close their eyes) Say the sentences and then repeat them.

For example,

My name is Arti. I am wearing a red dress today. I enjoy eating Ice-cream.

Then ask questions like

(a) What is my name ?

(b) What is the colour of my dress ?
(c) What am I eating ?

My Observation

The students were able to answer the questions as they think that they are very simple. The students developed confidence when they found that they have answered the questions. These simple questions kick-started the students interest in Listening activity.

Next Day

The teacher speaks 3 or 4 very simple sentences of any chapter. I instruct students to close their books and close their eyes. Then I speak few sentences (the easiest ones) of the chapter that I am going to take up. Then I repeat the sentences and ask questions from the students.

The students tried to answer the question and gradually developed confidence.

I Contribute 5 minutes Everyday for My Listening Activity.

Benefits

Definitely, I have seen a remarkable improvement in my students. When we provide a comfortable environment to our students and nurture them with love, care and affection the roots of our relationship become strong and the shoot of child's personality soars high.

The students try their very best to combat their unwillingness and continue to move along the positive path. Previously hesitant students, trying to avoid English instructions, Now Felt Comfortable.

Conclusion

Creating a comfortable environment and sensitizing the students about the need to learn a language promotes a successful teaching and learning environment. I "genuinely" care for my students and guide them. I listen and observe my students, to know and understand them. I provide my First Generation Learners ample opportunities to listen to English Language.

The More you Listen, The Better you Communicate.

Connecting with my students provides me the opportunity of knowing how and when to address their specific needs. It is my responsibility to help guide my students to acquire the skills they need to succeed in school and in the real world.

I feel extremely Happy & Satisfied to see the Smile on the faces of my students, to feel the Warmth of their affection and to witness the Confidence in their personality. I teach Language and according to me, language is not just a combination of words and phrases to communicate. It depicts a whole culture. It is the beauty of the language to Connect people.

13

Some Innovative Practices in Teaching & Learning of English at Secondary Level

— Asha Khurana

Introduction

"If they cannot learn the way we teach, we teach the way they learn."

- O. Iver Lovass

Students love change. They learn better when the teacher changes her way of teaching. With this hypothesis in mind, the teacher develops innovative methods.

In Indian classrooms, traditional teaching methods[1] were followed for teaching English at school and university level. In such classrooms, teacher would act as a sage on the stage, who is a repository of knowledge and he would do all the talking in the classroom and poor students listen to him translating his lesson word by word, writing answers on the board, they copy the same in their notebooks and later they learn the same and produce in the exam. This was and still is in many classrooms methods of teaching English language. This results in no learning of English language.

Over the last three decades and so methods, approaches and techniques of teaching English have changed. Our teaching should be students centric. Language learning is skill development, hence the importance of practice and drill. There have been the direct methods of teaching and communicative approach of English language teaching. Then, they say the student is not a passive recipient of knowledge, so came the constructivist approach in English teaching. Next, the teacher is not an imparter of knowledge but 'a facilitator' 'a support by the side' and a 'co-learner' in the learning process.

In a language learning classroom, all the four skills of language learning listening, speaking, reading, writing should be given equal importance. Whereas in most of our classrooms reading & writing are given more importance over speaking & listening, hence, our students when come out of university fail to get jobs because they lack productive skills of the language.

In this 21st century, we are dealing with a different set of students who have technology in their hands in the form of smart devices like smartphones, tabs and laptops. Technology helps them to learn any concept and lesson without the help of a teacher or without going to the library.

Therefore, in the present age, the teacher who follows bookish knowledge or concepts does not excite the students. Theoretical concepts, which are available with the click of a mouse on their laptops, no more attract them to classrooms. Rote teaching and learning methods of yesteryears thus will never be able to stimulate today's students.

Hence, the need for innovative methods of teaching which stimulate and excite them and they learn the language and also develop useful skills in life. In this 21st century, teachers are required to impart or facilitate the acquisition of the 4 C's.[2] The 4 C's include:

- Communication
- Collaboration
- Creativity &
- Critical Thinking.

The Researcher has twenty-five years of experience of teaching English at secondary and senior secondary level. She has worked with students of different ability groups at different times. Methods, techniques and approaches followed were moulded as per the need of students and prevalent practices of those days. In this research paper, the researcher wishes to discuss and illustrate the innovative methods and techniques which she practiced in her classrooms and which produced good results in the form of students improved language abilities.

This innovative action research that she aims to present here was carried out on 160 students who were spread over in 4 classes consisting of 40 students each. Students are in the age group of 15-17 years. They are in similar ability group and are passably at a good level of English language. Practices are being followed for the last two years and are still in progress.

I. Mindfulness

Mindfulness practice with 11th & 12th grade students in the school of excellence –

> Essentially mindfulness is a way of being in the present moment, noticing what you are experiencing with compassion & without judgment. The benefits are increased concentration & engagement, improvement in attention span, focus, compassion and self — esteem.

As the researcher has already learnt & practiced VIPASSANA[3] and has a conviction that it will work for her students too. Class XI students of 2018-19 batch were given regular brief sessions of this for a month & so. They used to have an English period of 40 minutes right after the lunch break. In that class, it was found that they were restless, disinterested with lots of goofy energy & their minds wandering.

Mindfulness practice in the class for initial five minutes was initiated where they were first made aware of the sounds of the surrounding, then were made to relax their body parts one by one and finally practice ANAPANA[4] breathing technique of VIPASSANA. They concentrate on their breathing, natural breath without tampering with it. They were made to practice for five to ten minutes and then they were made to open their eyes and target chapter started thereafter.

No doubt, it was a loss of time as there was huge syllabus to cover but the look of calmness on their faces, focus and concentration with which they worked later, helped in persisting with the practice.

In this academic year 2019-20, Education Department of Delhi has introduced Entrepreneur Curriculum[5] in all government run Schools. Under that also they are given the regular practice of mindfulness in classes. In a usual class of forty students observation is that 25 students like the sessions. Their improved behaviour and their academic output are the indication that practices are helping them.

II. Innovative Ways of Vocabulary Building

Secondary level students already possess good vocabulary and usage of correct tenses. To help them build a good active vocabulary their textbook is used as a medium in one such practice. They are taught Graphic Organiser[6] to learn and retain their vocabulary. One such graphic organiser is FRAYER Model.[7]

Classroom lessons are taught by giving them the dictionary meaning of the words in the context of the lesson. For some words, they are asked to put them in a FRAYER model, which goes like this:[8]

In another instance, In an English club meeting, it was taken in the form of an activity, where each student of the group had to bring a new word for the group and present the same through FRAYER Model to the group. Thus, enhancing the vocabulary of the group.

In another activity, a teacher randomly picks words from the text lessons and asks from the class, like a 'vocab quiz'. They have to tell the context in which the word appeared in the lesson and in which text lesson it is mentioned. Those who are unable to figure out have to read the chapters again and try to find out. This works as a revision of the lesson and enhances their vocabulary.

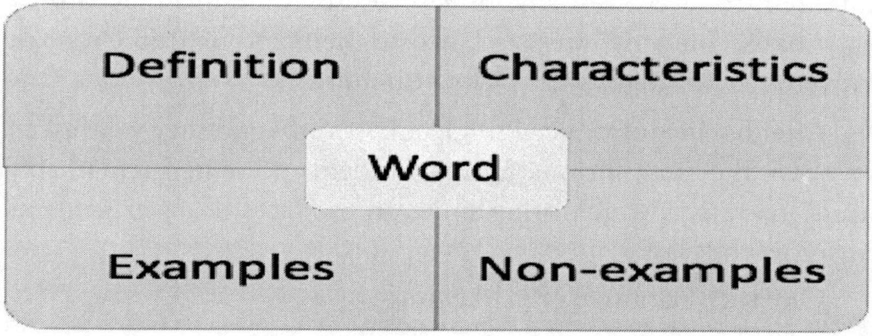

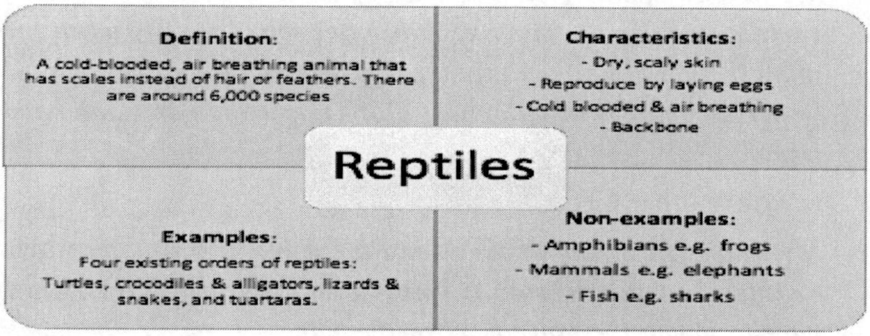

As an extension, even in the next class, they are asked questions about previous class vocabulary. They make mental connections and try to retain and make it a part of their active vocabulary by using it in a different context.

III. Proverbs of English Language and Weaving them into Narratives

In olden times, when grammar-translation method was adopted to teach English, students used to get sentences and paragraph in Hindi and were supposed to translate it in English. In that, they would get proverbs of Hindi language to translate it in English. Later on, with the direct method of teaching English, this method of teaching through translation stopped and students do not possess the knowledge of proverbs of the English language.

Present-day students are lacking in their proverbial knowledge and hence the teaching and learning of proverbs in my classes were reintroduced. Initially, three proverbs were introduced on a daily basis. The same was explained to them and used in contexts. Proverbs to be taught were picked carefully.

After having introduced some ten proverbs and they were asked to weave the same into narratives. Students presented remarkably funny narratives which bring smile on the faces of other students sitting in the class.

One such narrative goes like this:

My mother always gives me a lot of work to do and whenever I refuse to do it, she says like father like son. One day when my younger sister did a huge mistake, I took it on me and was scolded by my parents. My situation was 'give a dog a bad name and hang it too.

In one another piece:

My studies in School of Excellence are going so far so good. My eleventh and twelfth class is going to be very tough, therefore I have to follow the proverb when the going gets tough, the tough get going.

IV. Use of Newspaper to Teach English

Newspapers are cheap, easily available, authentic and useful resource, which can be used liberally in an English teaching class.

- Newspapers have certain advantages over textbooks like textbooks do not contain new material and students get bored with them after some time. Newspapers are fresh and loaded with new information each day.
- Newspapers reflect developments in the language styles and also it helps students and teachers to be abreast of them.
- Newspapers are linguistically updated and provide valuable linguistic inputs.
- The newspaper reports real-life events and arouses students curiosity.

Newspapers are an invaluable source of authentic material, the more students read, the more they want to explore. As the newspapers are many and have vast information teacher has to be careful with the way to organise a certain activity around them.

In class 11th and 12th newspapers are related to curriculum. Students of class xi and xii have advanced writing skills in their curriculum. Under this they have to learn to prepare classified advertisements, invitations, posters, write reports of events and accidents and write articles too.

Examination pattern tasks are taken up in the class with them one by one. The first step is: It is explained to them: what a classified ad is and how does it look like. Next step is: back home, they should pick up any random newspaper of English language, and study classified columns, cut and paste some classified ads in their notebooks. Next day in the class, they are asked to observe essential features of such classified ads. They are made to write/ enlist those in their notebooks.

Next, they are given handouts where they have mixed type of classified ads and they are asked to segregate them into different columns. This is done as a group activity. In yet another activity, they are having newspaper advertisements as a model, they are given questions and asked to prepare classified advertisements.

The same process with little variation is adopted for teaching them to **prepare invitations and posters**. Newspapers are replete with such things. They collaborate and work in pairs or in small groups.

For report writing, some sample reports, carefully selected from newspaper, are brought in the class, given to them to read and then discussion about its format and essential features follow. They observe & write reports of some other similar event, teacher facilitate the task and keep on helping them to fill the gaps in their work. This becomes a take-off stage, next they are given assignments to prepare for examination.

V. Using Textbooks to Develop Critical Thinking Skills and Creativity

It was during one training session by British Council on surface learning & deep learning that the researcher learnt about core skills of 21st century and need to inculcate the same in learner and how it can be embedded in their curriculum.

These core skills are as follow: critical thinking & problem solving, creativity and imagination, digital literacy, student leadership & personal development & communication.

Inculcation of the skill of creativity, critical thinking and problem solving depended upon questioning techniques of the teacher, (which was majorly Socratics method)[9] in class. Does the teacher ask closed questions or open-ended questions? Closed questions have fixed answers. They are remembering, recall and comprehension questions whereas open questions have many answers. Open questions force the child to classify, organize, evaluate and come up with convincing valid points. They learn to relate their leanings to their previous knowledge, make connections and share with others.

Bloom's taxonomy[10] that talks about lower-order thinking skills & higher-order thinking skills is followed while framing questions. Questions posed should look like this:

- Can you guess what will happen?
- Can give me an example? Can you find another example?
- Is this the same as ……? Is this different from?
- What connections can you see between….?
- What other ways there to ….?
- What is wrong with ….?
- Can you group these?
- Can you explain this to your partner?
- What would happen if ….?
- What always seem to happen?

- What alternative would you suggest for…?
- Compose a poem on the same lines…?
- Is there a better solution…?

Textbook lessons were reviewed from the angle of embedding thinking, critical thinking & creative questions. Questions posed ranged from LOTS to HOTS. Every question was planned before going to the class. Lesson plans moved on this cycle.

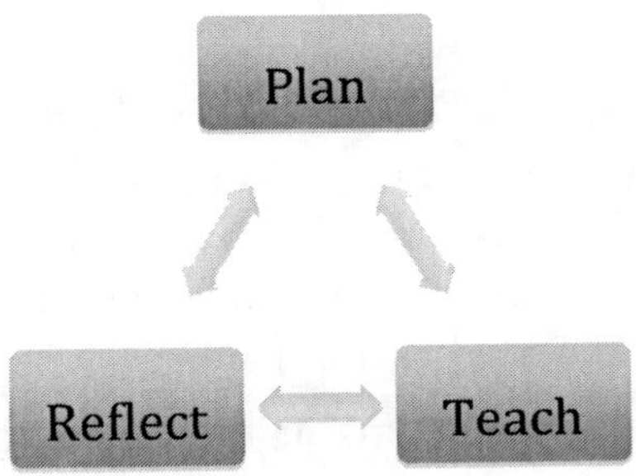

When it was practiced with the students, there were certain problems. Students have not been taught to interpret, analyze, classify and evaluate in their earlier classes. They are in the habit of taking teacher's words as gospel truth. Initially, they find it difficult but a teacher has to persist in her efforts and they start working on the lines.

The first step with students was to motivate them to think beyond the text, the next step was to motivate them to share with their peers and with the larger group too. One common daily activity in the class used to be: think-pair-share.

To reach to the level of critical thinking they are taught its sub-skills like comprehend interpret, classify, analyze, evaluate through carefully crafted activities and questions. One such activity that was taught to them and they religiously followed was to prepare theme cards of characters and events of the lessons done in the class.

While preparing such cards in their notebooks, they read the text, analyze the utterances and actions of character concerned & come up with some adjectives for them. Its structure run like this:

Sl. No.	*Name of the character*	*Physical appearance*	*Qualities of Character*	*Role*	*Problems faced, if any*

Students read a poem from their textbook, after all the discussion related to its interpretation and study of poetic devices they are motivated to compose one on the lines. The activity works well in my classroom. I have got many compositions from my students.

In one of the chapters, narrator is describing his village in detail in a humorous way. Students are assigned the task of describing their hometown. Students are taught Venn diagram, Timeline, flow chart, Mind Map, Web chart, foldable and many other Graphic Organizers as per the need of the chapter.

There still persist problems in the classroom. With all such activities,students thinking process is sparked, they have ideas, they want to share but they lack expressions. They are motivated to share in non-threatening atmosphere, they are helped with the expression and in dire need a word or two of Hindi language can be used in the class.

Conclusion

Students of the 21st century are not the same as the students of the 20th century. There is an onslaught of technology in every field of their lives. Their education is not the same as the education of 20th-century students was. As a teacher we have new challenges to face, wes have to move with the times. In a way, teachers too are learning & growing with their students. Teachers need to be abreast of all the new things in the field of teaching, learning and should not shy away from practicing new things.

The teacher observes the impact of new practices on his students, reflect on this techniques & methods, again; plan and carry out his teaching. The cycle goes on and on.

Students always want change and any new thing in the class makes them take interest in studies. Once they get interested and involved, half the battle is won. Hence everyday lesson should be planned with some new element in it. It can be some activity, pair work, group work & so on. Whatever is taken up with the students should have a clearly defined objective, which must result in learning outcome. Teaching and learning can become an enjoyable activity and fun in the hands of the resourceful and innovative teacher. As regards innovations, there is no limit to it. Many teachers all over the world are working and teaching innovatively to which we sitting here are unaware.

Notes

1. Traditional Methods of Teaching English involve: Grammar Transaltion Method; Direct Method and Audio Linguial Method. for further reading see, http://www.nzdl.org/gsdlmod?e=d-00000-00---off-0hdl--00-0----0-10-0---0---0direct-10---4-------0-1l--11-en-50---20-about---00-0-1-00-0--4----0-0-11-10-0utfZz-8-10&cl=CL2.7.11&d=HASHf4c763bbedf2771100d30b.4.1&gt=1
2. Blog: What Are the 4 C's of 21st Century Skills? availabe at: https://www.aeseducation.com/career-readiness/what-are-the-4-cs-of-21st-century-skills
3. Editorial, India Today, January 15, 2018; available at: https://www.indiatoday.in/lifestyle/health/story/what-exactly-is-vipassana-the-meditation-technique-president-kovind-swears-by-1145720-2018-01-15
4. Dr. K.S. Ayyar, The Value of Anapana and Vipassana in psychological and psychosomatic illness; available at: https://www.vridhamma.org/research/The-Value-of-Anapana-and-Vipassana-in-psychological-and-psychosomatic-illnesses
5. Staff Reporter, Govt launches entrepreneurship curriculum for school students; available at: https://www.unido.org/our-focus/creating-shared-prosperity/agribusiness-and-rural-entrepreneurship-development/entrepreneurship-curriculum-programme
6. Graphic Organisers, British Council of India available at: https://www.teachingenglish.org.uk/article/graphic-organisers
7. National Behaviour Support Service, *Frayer Model*, available at: https://www.nbss.ie/sites/default/files/publications/frayer_model_-_vocbulary_strategy_handout__copy_3.pdf
8. This picture, for illustration taken from: https://www.theconfidentteacher.com/2018/04/vocabulary-knowledge-and-the-frayer-model/

9. Socratic Teaching, available at: https://www.criticalthinking.org/pages/socratic-teaching/606
10. Bloom's Taxonomy of Learning Domains, available at: http://www.nwlink.com/~donclark/hrd/bloom.html

14

Setting Benchmark for Learning, Teaching and Assessment for English Language in Indian Education System

— *Pradeep Sharma*

Introduction

In a globalized economy, English communicative skills have great significance wherein India is a key business player. The demand is going to increase without doubt. Today 20% of the world population is using English as a first and second language combined. There was huge resistance towards use of English, half a century back in countries like Germany, China, Japan and Russia but gradually most countries have come on the same page to acquire global skills. As far as India is concerned, only about 12% population can speak English which is around little more than 50% of average of total world English speakers. Moreover, English as a language used by Indians does not have a required standard in terms of production quality i.e. spoken or written. There are several reasons but one of the major reasons for this is indifferent attitude towards learning the language systematically.

Sources of English Language in India

Primary source of learning English in India are schools and colleges where majority of teachers/lecturers lack English language skills, curriculum is not standard, and there is a lack of trained teachers with varied approach to pedagogy. Even in English medium private schools, teachers have mediocre skills. Barring small percentages of elite schools, teachers engaged as language teachers, do not have required proficiency in English. There are government funded public schools where most of the teachers do not know English, except the language teacher. Even the language teachers have mostly grammatical skills but do not have spoken or communicative proficiency. Due to privatisation in education, private schools are mushrooming today in India. There are private schools which are franchise schools which do better in terms of quality as they have regular teacher's training programme. As these schools charge hefty fee, they are able to hire qualified and experienced staff with better English learning proficiency. However, most staff in these schools still do not have C1 or C2 level language proficiency on CEFR levels. Private budget schools without the network branches fail to hire qualitative manpower with good proficiency in English. Focus of such school is on cost-cutting and profit generation. As a result there is hardly any investment on teacher's capacity building. This definitely affects the learning of students as the teachers are not well trained for transferring language proficiency in their students.

This language proficiency skill gap has given rise to activation of private coaching classes where students try to fill the learning gaps in terms of English speaking. Many of these coaching centres prepare students for taking International Testing Systems viz. IELTS, TOEFL, PTE, and Life skills exams which measure the proficiency of non-native speakers. Approximately 0.4 million people appear for these international testing systems to immigrate or study abroad involving huge personal investment. However, their contribution does not benefit India directly or indirectly as they aspire to move out of the country. Presence of spoken English coaching classes will not have a major impact on the change in this scenario. Hence, we need to bank only on the education system for acquisition and development of global skills in India.

Emphasis on Multi-language approach in Educational Framework of 2019

Though, the new educational framework reform of 2019 rightly lays emphasis that mother tongue should be promoted as the child is pragmatically more comfortable in learning through first language. Indian languages are quite rich in lexis and therefore unnecessary obsession should be avoided by parents. The policy does acknowledge that scientific & technological studies are only possible through English. Moreover, it is a leading language for transaction worldwide and therefore it should not be ignored. English is also required for local interactions within the country as only 45% people speak Hindi in India. A Gujarati gentleman travelling in southern India may face difficulty in business transactions or tour as proportion of Hindi speakers are less.

Many countries have protected their own language and made higher studies possible in their language. Thus, it will be a great idea that India gives priority to its own language by standardizing its learning along with English. Hence, research should be initiated in this direction so that all languages are assessed on the quality criteria of language rather than today's achievement based assessment.

Need for setting bench mark

Setting bench mark by devising a framework for developing learning pedagogy is bound to improve the standard of any language. The current language learning and assessment is not task based. Literature learning and communicative languages are two different aspects but may complement each other in learning process. Hence, there is a need for setting objective oriented bench mark for learning, teaching and assessment of English language. The framework can also be used for other Indian languages as well.

English as a cultural and traditional carrier

English as a global language is certainly a cultural carrier for our tradition to spread across the globe. In the last few decades, Yoga and Ayurveda are two recent traditional systems of wellness and medicines which have found space in people's heart across the world. Lot of foreign students come to India in order to study our ancient medicine systems. It is only English through which they can be initially taught before they learn Sanskrit. Likewise, our research students would be able to translate our literary treasure to be read worldwide only in English if they acquire sound language skills. If the quality of translation or writing is not standard, it will fail to reach appropriately to the world audience. UGC has pointed out recently on the quality of research work in the recent past. So, along with our Indian languages, we need to promote English also. Hence, we must try to improve the standard of learning through appropriate pedagogies. We also need to define the outcomes, so that teaching, learning and assessment can be integrated.

Albert Einstein had said "India is great grandmother of tradition". But in the absence of effective medium of language, our rich cultural heritage is never going to reach its destination. Transliteration work can be strengthened only when our young minds are given good knowledge of regional language knowledge along with English language knowledge in terms of reception and production (listening, reading, writing and speaking). We must not have any threat for weakening of our language because of dominance of English language. Rather, we should promote and showcase our literary work to the world by translating it in English language. Indian philosophy, literature, traditions are undoubtedly rich and cannot be shadowed by English language. However, aspiration of Indians to see India as world teacher is never going to materialise if we do not emphasise quality learning of English language.

Obsession Vs Requirement of English

Whether it is our obsession or do we really require English language is highly debatable question. "Learn English but don't be English" is a great quote in this context. Parents in India are quite obsessed today that their children study in English Medium schools. Is this trend a result of superfluous mindset or is based on right perceptions? This would need critical analysis. It is undeniable fact that information technology uses English as a front-end language. In the absence of knowledge of English, an individual is definitely going to find it difficult. Instructions in the software are also in English. Secondly, most private organisations use English as a language of business communication and make it mandatory for job seekers to have operational knowledge of English. Lack of knowledge of English affects the employability factor of job seekers to a great extent. Companies are compelled to use English as they have to maintain trading or business relations. As the government jobs are below 5% of the total share of market jobs, realisation of the fact that a person should know good English is not wrong. Due to globalisation, more and more companies are trading with foreign companies for exports and imports. Thus, education in vernacular language is considered to be risky by parents in long run as it would impact employability. Also, today most tertiary education takes place in English language. So far as adaptability is concerned, switching over to English medium after 10+2 becomes even more difficult alternative. As language learning is a set of larger part of demand and supply, it would be inappropriate to say that parents' push for English is obsessive act. The perceptions of parents seem to have been built over a period of time from the above facts.

Why to standardize English language?

India has derived its constitutional features from various countries like Canada, USA, France, Germany, and South Africa. We are using foreign technology. Our education system is also taking pedagogical inputs from various countries in modifying curriculum, learning and teaching methodologies. This has certainly opened the door for improvement and innovations. Then why not take a cue from the research work of European frameworks. A lot of research has been done in the field of preparing language framework in

Europe by creating Common European Framework of Reference for languages (CEFR) which can be applied and made basis for learning any language. This does not mean glorification of foreign language but applying CEFR researches to our advantage. Our rich cultural heritage in form of Indian language should certainly get the precedence. Standardizing our own languages and setting benchmark for Hindi and other regional language would also be a great initiative. Hence, taking cues from CEFR, we can certainly devise our own framework which will help to improve the quality of English and Indian languages.

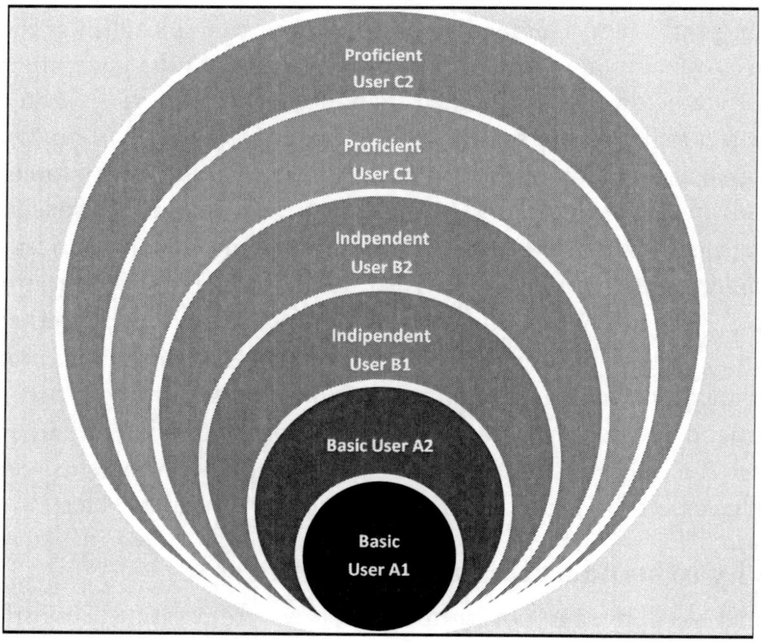

Figure 1: (CEFR Levels hierarchy)

CEFR (The common European Framework of references for Languages: learning teaching and assessment) is a framework used to evaluate achievements of learners of foreign language initially used across Europe and increasingly in other countries. It was published by the *modern languages division of the council of Europe* in 2001 after a period of research from 1993 to 1999. It is becoming globally accepted norms for learning, teaching and evaluation. The CEFR provides a general framework which indicates what language learners need to learn to be able to use a foreign language effectively in practice, thereby creating a common basis for language learning curricula or guidelines, qualifications, textbooks, examinations, and syllabuses across European states. The CEFR is based on an action-oriented approach to language learning and use. It includes six proficiency levels for foreign language learning for all components viz. Listening, Reading, Speaking and Writing. CEFR elaborately describes all the six proficiency levels. Many Asian countries have taken initiative in last decade to standardize their language learning process.

Experiments of using CEFR to standardise English in other countries

As the CEFR originated in Europe and was made by the council of Europe, it has been implemented fully and partially by the member countries. Many other countries have endeavoured to take cues from it and reformed their national language curriculum. Many Asian countries have begun to align their English language learning framework with CEFR in last decade with credible impact on improving their English language proficiency index.

(a) **CEFR alignment in Malaysia (CEFR-M):** As a result of language based reforms, Malaysia moved to 14th position out of 70 countries with high English proficiency in a survey by EF English Proficiency Index. This is dramatic rise in proficiency building in any nation. Malaysia (CEFR-M) started implementing its version in various phases. In first phase (2013-2015) they focused on raising the level of English proficiency of teachers. In the next phase (2016) in first part they matched educational levels from pre-schools to teacher education with the CEFR levels. While in the second part of Phase 2, School Based Assessment (SBA), syllabus and curricula were also aligned with CEFR descriptors (National Education Blueprint, 2013). Finally, in third phase they focussed on creating ELSQC (English Language Standards and Quality Council) to evaluate, review and revise the implementation of CEFR.

(b) **CEFR alignment in China (CSE – China's Standard of English Language Ability)**: (National Education Examinations Authority (NEEA) in China took great leap by taking initiative to set Standards by developing China's Standards of English Language Ability (CSE) in 2018 through a national framework of reference for English language education. It is important to note that the management structure of education in China had different governmental departments which took charge of education at different stages. The main challenge before the policy makers was that there was inconsistent learning objectives specified in the curricula for learning of English at each educational stage. To counter second challenge, reflecting proficiency levels aligned to the curriculum at each stage, national tests were developed and administered by different testing organizations. This led to development of a common English proficiency scale to facilitate testing and score interpretation by tailoring CEFR to suit the need. The new system was made more transparent enough for outside world. As a significant achievement of research and collaborative efforts, finally China is able successfully map their CSE evaluation to IELTS, APTIS and TOEFL.

(c) **Vietnam: CEFR-V:** The Vietnamese Ministry of Education and Training (MOET) took great initiative in 2008 by defining their English language benchmark and adopted CEFR. It was from primary through the tertiary levels of education. The objective was to achieve B1 level by all university graduates other than language were expected by 2020 as a national project. However, survey in 2015 revealed that 20% objective was only achieved. The reasons were teacher's poor English, lack of resources and outdated grammar intensive teaching pedagogy. The government has reinitiated and revisited objectives of the learning and teaching plans. The new approach is undertaken by creating CEFR-V, a Vietnamese version, resembling Japanese version CEFR-J. The new framework is adjusted to make it more suitable for Vietnamese studying foreign languages. There is greater focus on training teachers of English.

(d) **Thailand (FRELE-TH):** A massive survey on 40,000 teachers was conducted by Thailand government which revealed that proficiency level of teachers was found to be low. Majority of teachers could only achieve beginner's level only. Thailand ranks 53rd among 80 non-native speaking countries on proficiency index (2017). Under the aegis English Language Institute (ELI), a branch of the Ministry of Education (MOE), took initiative in April 2014 by announcing a policy that all aspects of English language curriculum reform was to be aligned with CEFR framework. Hence, a local version of CEFR named FRELE-TH (2018) was published including Evaluation and Accreditation of Quality Language Services (EAQUALS). The FRELE-TH has two scale types to describe the English proficiency levels: a global scale (overall descriptors) and illustrative scales, (communicative activities, communication strategies, and communicative language competence). The rationale behind the development of FRELE-TH lies in the principle of CEFR's inception that CEFR does not offer ready-made solutions but must be adapted to the requirements of particular contexts. In order to meet these objectives a 10-level reference framework was developed as an adaptation of CEFR to make it relevant to English use in local and international communication in Thailand. It was expected that the FRELE-TH is calibrated with the CEFR to meet the global scale for standardized tests of English proficiency.

Challenges related with implementation of CEFR in India

India being geographically and culturally diverse nation has more challenges than other countries in implementation or aligning CEFR with the curriculum. There are 22 official languages as per eighth schedule of Indian Constitution. Education is also a concurrent subject as per the constitution on which both state and centre make policies. There are two secondary/senior secondary education boards namely CBSE & ICSE along with 29 state boards. So, since the stake holders are too many, consensus may not be so easy. First thing is to find its place in national education policy so that our own version of CEFR can be formulated. Following issues are associated with the implementation:

(a) Education being a concurrent subject, policy decisions are difficult.

(b) Consensual issues by stakeholders viz. centres, states, education boards etc.

(c) The traditional resistance to change and adaptation to CEFR.

(d) Training teachers for the new challenges on new benchmark.

(e) Teachers having very limited knowledge and exposure to CEFR.

(f) Teachers‘ level of English proficiency.

(g) Lack of local CEFR experts who are willing to contribute to change.

Possible Impact of setting benchmark for learning, teaching and Assessment

Benchmark will certainly pave the way for standardizing the learning, teaching and assessment in India resulting in improved overall language proficiency Index of India. This will impact improved employability and skilled manpower to meet the globalized market demands.

Road-map for CEFR

- In first stage, experts should be engaged to carry out detailed feasibility study to formulate language benchmark suitable for India on the line of CEFR.
- Secondly, assess the requirement of resources, and implementation modalities.
- Thirdly, engage teachers for training under the new language benchmark
- Devise curriculum and learning pedagogies
- Create a language assessment authority for implementation.

Conclusion

The implementation of CEFR is bound to have innumerable challenges as it would need lot of reforms involving various stakeholder viz. Policy framers, administrators, teachers etc. It would be very challenging to implement CEFR directly. However, using it indirectly by embedding its features for obtaining outcome would be a better option. We can customize CEFR suitable to our need.

Works Cited

Council of Europe: Modern Language Division. *Common European Framework of References for Languages: Teaching, Learning and Assessment (CEFR).* Cambridge University Press, 2001.pdf

Little, David. "State of the art article: The Common European Framework of References for Languages: Content, Purpose, Origin, Reception and Impact". *Cambridge journals,* 2006, doi :10.1017/S0261444806003557.pdf

Ministry of Human Resource Development, Government of India. *National Education Policy draft, 2019.*pdf

National Council of Educational Research and Training. *Teaching of English: Position Paper, National Focus Group.* 1st., ed New Delhi, March 2006.pdf

Foley, J.A. "Issues on Assessment using CEFR in the Region". *LEARN Journal: Language Education and Acquisition Research Network Journal,* Vol. 12, No. 2, The Graduate School of Human Sciences, Assumption University, Thailand jfoley@au.edu, July 2019.Pd

Appendices

Abstracts

Use of Language Games in Bangladeshi EFL Classroom for Practicing Speaking: Prospects & Challenges

— Md. Sadequle Islam,

In South Asia, English is taught as a foreign language and English teaching in EFL (English as Foreign Language) context is quite a big challenge. The success in learning any language at first can be perceived from the capacity of the learner's speaking. But to be very specific, students are often reluctant to speak in English. Apart from mentioning some successful language games, this paper also aims to find out the teachers' and students' perceptions including prospects and challenges concerning the use of language games for practicing speaking skill and their impact on the language learners. The results indicate that though games in Bangladeshi EFL classroom maximize positive result on the frequency of English speaking practice, there are lack of logistic supports and goodwill of some teachers as well as authorities that results hindrance to the use of games in Bangladeshi EFL classroom.

Empowered Learning of English Language: A Pragmatic Deconstruction

— *Garima Bhayana*

The term "inclusion" has a wide spectrum of not only the kinds of learners but also significantly holds the fact that language learning happens through unlimited sources as well as processes. The following paper attempts to deconstruct those processes that can turn into techniques in the disguise of vernacular methods with the objective of sharing, in place of dictating knowledge. This paper is also a trial to decode how some highly effective language learning activities work positively on school and college students. It mentions some realtime observations from a class of specially-abled learners (CWSN) followed by insights directly from a practising Special Educator. Additionally, the paper aims to pay special attention to unconventional digital catalysts that aid in contextual learning such as illustrations and multimedia. It focuses on cultural and "concrete" learning ways that work on the habit development part of one's mind, associating the biological functioning of one's neuroscientific phenomena with "basal ganglia".

Encapsulating responses from the current generation of school, college children as well as one of the influential illustrators of children's books, this paper concludes with an amalgamation of my own teaching experience with the help of authentic and exhilarating exercises. A correlation of one's first language acquisition with the second language is that music, songs and mnemonics play an imperative role in emerging as "tools" to pushing grammatical rules and verbose into the learners' long term evocation, withal.

The Graphic Novel as an Innovative Teaching Methodology in Higher Education

— ***Priyanka Charan***

The graphic novel represents a new and current state of the comics industry. Recent studies have revealed the great educational potential of comics. However, scientific literature on their use in the university setting is virtually non-existent. The present paper aims to promote the use of graphic novel as an innovative teaching methodology with a great potential in higher education, and to present and assess the experience conducted in the Physiotherapy degree program. Students would be provided with series of graphic novels that take an entertaining and practical look at the social healthcare reality of distinct pathologies. Along with discussions and debates that will be conducted in class, an individual reflective work will be carried out in writing by students, in which they would be expressing their satisfaction regarding this methodology. Based on our experience, the graphic novel should be considered an innovative teaching methodology with a great potential in higher education.

Keywords: Innovative teaching; Higher Education; Graphic novel; Physiotherapy.

Shifting from Quantitative Assessment to Qualitative Assessment of Language Skills in India

— ***Nidhi Pradeep Sharma***

English as a common connective language has acquired immense prominence in the last few decades in India. The prime reason for this standing lies in historical dominance by the native English speakers under the colonial rule. Advances in the information technology field and globalization has further proliferated its use. It was initially considered as an advantageous skill but today English is considered as a basic ability. Teaching and learning of English, especially in schools & colleges in India has revolved around literary text and assessments are mostly quantitative in nature which does not meet the modern language skills requirements. Academic approach towards learning, teaching and assessment of English as a language in India lacks a holistic approach towards properly defined objectives of achievements. For a better teaching and learning, it is imperative to define the measurable outcomes rather subjectively. There is a need to define goals which are based on action oriented proficiency level measurement instead of current one which are based on achievement oriented based on quantitative grading. In fact, marks or grades do not reveal practical proficiency level of a person. Once the outcome parameters of assessment are described, teaching and learning approaches, processes and modalities can easily be defined for all components of language viz. listening, speaking reading and writing. This would leave greater room for innovations. Thinking of innovations without thinking of outcomes would be futile. This paper shall discuss issues related to current evaluation pattern with a paradigm shift in assessment approach. It would also outline a suggestive approach towards assessment of English language skills which would leave a larger scope for innovative teaching & learning of English in schools and colleges in India.

Setting Benchmark for Learning, Teaching and Assessment for English Language in Indian Education System

— ***Pradeep Kumar Sharma***

The growing need for common language i.e. English in the globalized economy is ever increasing and there is imperative need for standardising the language proficiency to meet global standards.

Around one tenth of India's young population can manage to converse or use English. The source of learning English is mainly through formal education at schools which are divided into various kinds of boards having different approaches to learning, teaching and assessment. Until there is a standardized approach, proficiency building is a farfetched goal. The struggle of English learners can be visible when they have to take international testing exams like IELTS, TOEFL, PTE etc which are mapped to Common European Reference of Languages: Learning, Teaching and Assessment, a frame used to describe achievements of foreign learners. This gap in question can only be filled if we either map our language learning to CEFR or devise our own improvised system. This research paper will focus on brief study of the existing language learning, teaching and assessment and suggest reforms with possible impacts and bring innovation to the language learning standards. It will also suggest whether standardization would be feasible for institutions (school /college) in rural areas due to lack of trained teachers from the researcher's long experience of imparting English language teaching.

Audiovisual Aids and Real Life Experiences in Language Learning

— ***Smriti Ashra***

My paper will focus on how audio-visual methods impact learning of a language, particularly English. The paper will also investigate how novels and movies impact the learning as well as the understanding of a language and its background. It will mainly focus on how an English classroom is supposed to be surrounded by techniques, that are supposed to act as guiding principles for the efficient teaching of the language. Moreover, the paper will try to enlighten the assessment ideas that could be interesting and creative along with focusing on the kind of learning that will stay for a lifetime.* This will also contribute in the analysis of how things are important to be known and experienced that will be beyond the bookish knowledge.* The paper will try to focus on the creative yet contributing aspects of the learningfield process i.e. the field trips , educational tours and excursions as a medium especially for understanding text and it's background that often gets a little boring with the hefty reading. This paper will try to connect and bridge the gap between any textual knowledge to the practicality of the subject and the remembrance; this will act as a perfect base for judging ones work and will help in the growth of students from school as well as college. The main focus of the paper will be on how one teacher can make learning easy, fun and long lasting for the learners who are curious yet confused but can surely find the direction of their interest if given proper guidance, efficient teacher as well as the effective support of the audio visual technology and other creative options.

Bridging gap: English as a Medium and English as a Language- An Anthropological Study

— ***Nayeema***

English language has emerged as a medium to break the barriers of communication gap in space and time. The language has crossed the borders of its original home tract because the scientific literature is mainly available in English medium. Many of the nontraditional speakers are trapped in distinguishing English as a medium of discipline and English as discipline. A study conducted in the selected schools of district Budgam, Kashmir reveals some contrasting inquisitiveness of the school children. Presently, eighty eight percent of the rural schools and 92% of the urban schools teach in English medium exclusively. Fifteen years back 54% of the rural schools and 61% of the urban schools had English as a medium of teaching. Interestingly, the guardians of school children believe that most of the present generation of English medium school children lack conceptual clarity in comparison to the students of same schools having studied in vernacular medium earlier. An observation conducted revealed, 64% of the secondary school students in urban areas were unable to understand the contents of the subject in English language while the percentage in rural areas is as much as 67%. More than 90% of the students in the selected schools cram the contents without proper understanding. Majority of the parents and guardians however believe that the new generation students are far better English speakers than the earlier ones. In addition there is progressive improvement in the learning of English language. Innovative curriculum, early focus of the language skills and vernacular medium up to middle school level can prevent the trap of their inability to distinguish the purpose of the subject of enquiry.

Approaches to English Language Teaching-Learning

— Dr. Valaria Sethi

The English language has many aspects which are to be given equal weightage in the teaching process. Many researches in the field of teaching methodology have been done and various methods, devices and techniques have been evolved. But it is fact that not a single method or technique is useful in teaching all aspects of language. The teacher has to follow the many sided approach in teaching one topic. The same topic can be taught by different methods and techniques at different levels. Some words can be introduced with the situational approach, whereas some words can be introduced by grammar-translation method. While teaching prose and poetry, teacher has to use different techniques. Anyhow fourfold skills of language learning must be achieved by many approaches. Reading, Writing, Speaking, Listening, and doing things. It was the first half of the present century, the teaching of English as a foreign language emerged as an autonomous profession. This was basically the result of a change in the perception of the role of English in post-colonial societies. The assumption behind the curriculum in the nineteenth century was that the objective of such a study would be the assimilation of British culture through the medium of English literature, in the early twentieth century, there emerged the notion of English as a second language, with a utilitarian function in the communication of knowledge. Nowadays, English has started to be recognized as a part of the local literary and cultural tradition of post- colonial societies because of its use in imaginative and creative contexts. The approach to English language teaching (in terms of curriculum, materials, etc.) has also necessarily had to change in view of these changes in the perception of the role of English. Due to research in various techniques in the field of language learning and teaching some classroom techniques as methods or approaches were adopted to teach English. Due to changing form and the status of English, many methods and approaches have been adopted to teach this language. The shortcomings of one method or approach give birth to another method or approach. To achieve the objectives of English teaching, the teacher must adopt the adequate method or approach. This paper aims at scrutinizing various approaches to English language teaching and learning.

Cinematic Literature and Reading Films: Visual Representation as a Medium of Instruction

— ***Swasti Sharma***

James Monaco in The Language of Film: Signs and Syntax asserted unlike English or French, a film has no idiosyncratic perspicuous 'langue'. Nevertheless, the absence of difference between signifier and signified enables limitless artistic freedom. Spectacle produced by a film precedes the faculty of speech. Therefore, one can infer that it is not necessary to acquire intellectual or linguistic competence to appreciate cinema. The contemporary university curriculum framework of graduate course in English offers insights into cinematic adaptations of texts . Perhaps the intention remains a smooth transition from the rudimentary understanding of film as a source of entertainment to a more nuanced comprehension of cinema as a Horatian didactic exercise. The research paper will attempt to examine the feasibility of teaching English literature through films and the challenges which accompany it. The paper will explore the thematic connections-both broad and focused-between literature and film. It will furnish justification for the use of film in an English classroom, followed by a review of the literature-both theoretical and practical-focused on the use of film in the English classroom.

Cinematic adaptation is integral to popular culture and one must acknowledge it as a significant foundation of consciousness aimed at the development of a pedagogy that links school/ university acquired knowledge to the lived experiences of students. The paper shall highlight similarities in narrative styles and thematic underpinnings of both literature and film. The focal point of the paper shall remain a close textual /trans textual analysis of the innovative approaches adopted by contemporary academics in ESL/EFL countries for the study of not just the English language ,but also literature. The changing landscape of cinema and the undulating trajectory of the written word are also some of the ancillary concerns that would contour the discourse.

Keywords: langue, spectacle, didactic.

Study of Language Patterns - Reflective of State of Happiness

— Ms. Vandana, Dr. Dayal Pyari

Happiness is a universal phenomenon, seek every human being on this earth. Everyone wants to be in a happy state of mind and body. Human beings are gifted with the most refined mind having the capacity to think, feel and communicate. The capacity to communicate is the most blessed capability which human beings are enjoying the most. Human beings are given the capacity to understand and reciprocate the gestures and the meaning of words. Thoughts when are converted into words become the power which influence the prosperous state of any human being. Whatever is being thought and communicated through language, always affect our state of mind and body as the happiness is a harmonious combination of mind body and soul and so reflected through verbal and nonverbal expression to the world inside and the world outside. Somewhere it is related to our value system too. So, language plays an important role in staying in happy state of body, mind and soul. This research paper tries to study the language patterns of five teacher educators. The pre and post data was collected through sound recorder and note taking app which was given to them with a schedule of recording their oral and written expressions in a single day of twenty-four hours. After pretest on the basis of studying the language patterns of pre data, the intervention for changing the word and sentences was given and again post intervention data was collected with same method. The pre and post data was analyzed thematically based on the different themes of states of happiness. The major finding was that the language patterns could determine the state of happiness of a mind with most reliable precision. The language pattern also indicated that when some happiness interventions were conducted to these five persons, language patterns were different as per recorded data. This study indicates that language plays a very important and significant role in creating the state of happiness.

Keywords: Language patterns and Happiness

Plurality of Resources in English Language "Teaching and Learning" in Rural Areas

— ***Malvika Oberoi***

English proficiency is viewed across societal levels as a necessary skill for accessing the best educational and professional prospects. A majority of Indians believe in trans formative power of English language. Having known that 70% of India lives in villages, majority of the work force comes from rural areas. It becomes imperative that students of such areas are given equal opportunities to learn English. The urban-rural divide in teaching of English has to be bridged. It is possible only if a committed and honest approach is adopted. Having said that a rural student is equally competent to be proficient in English, and for this, the English teacher has to adopt innovative strategies in the classroom by using plurality of resources.

The present paper examines various resources with or without using technology to make teaching – learning process enjoyable and beneficial for both learners and teachers. Use of newspapers, magazines, advertisements, radio, T.V., computers, mobile phones, social media and internet for content creation and delivery for better understanding of English language are highlighted. Paper enumerates a number of ways to acquaint with English language as one of the skills which can be polished by practice using scattered resources and too at learner's own pace. The different skills required for good listening, speaking, reading and writing activities can be nurtured and improved by using available resources having their own unique advantages and disadvantages as mentioned in the paper.

Paper concludes that it is possible for every child to learn English in the most enjoyable manner if it is supplemented with the appropriate resources and effective pedagogy by classroom teacher.

Sustaining Literacy and Critical Thinking in Indian Government Schools: A Study on Teach For India's Immersive Learning Methodologies

— Amit Sharma

Teach For India, an extension of Teach for All global initiative, is a rigorous programme that aims to bridge the gap between quality education and socio-economic deterrents that government-run schools in India are facing today. It follows a well-researched critical pedagogy that is rooted in contextual and creative learning. It aims to instill a sense of critical thinking and leadership in children coming from economically weaker sections. In this research paper, I shed light on my experience as a Teach For India fellow to talk about how the usage of carefully constructed literary tools, such as Visualization and Sensory Stimulation Learning Theory, help students develop a sense of experiential learning.

Teaching literature to children who come from places where they struggle to grasp basic syntactic structure of English seems at first a misappropriated point to begin with. However, my experience informs me that it has the potential to create a fertile ground to begin working on mending low literacy rate- the first challenge one faces when teaching English. In this paper, I will talk about some of the methodologies I have used to create an immersive classroom environment for my students to help them develop and sustain an interest in learning. My research findings further relate the usage of sensory stimulation theory with an increase in Reading Comprehension levels of the students and increased attention span. Furthermore, the research points towards how visualization helps children in improving their basic grasp on concepts, learning new words, and helps them explore themes deeply. I would therefore argue that literature, when coupled with immersive pedagogy (such as sing-along lessons, play-acting, directed conversations in peer groups, etc.), can help strengthen techniques meant to increase classroom literacy levels that are often challenged by socio-economic factors the children face. It also inculcates a sense of self-expression, leadership, confidence in students.

Going Beyond the Textbooks: Using Proverbs in English Class

— Dr. Meena Sehrawat

Teachers of English we confine ourselves to boundaries – textbook is one and ignoring mother tongue of the child in English class in another. The emphasis of the present paper is that we should go beyond the boundaries and use proverbs in mother tongue and English to arrest the learners' involvement and interest. Literature is not only what we conveniently call story, poem, autobiography or whatsoever name we give to the written form. Literature is all around us. It may also exist in oral form. The English studies in the contemporary context will enrich our understanding if we care to extend the conventional boundary and include the proverbs which we find around us in every region we live in. These proverbs which are at finger tips of the people living in a particular region provide a window to the socio-cultural context of that particular region in addition to encapsulating the basic human truth. The study of proverbs can also help lend that element of interest and bonding to the study of English studies which is sadly missing in today's teaching. The study of the proverbs, can reveal how they form the basis of a resistance culture and are inherited wisdom and figuratively refer to the socio-cultural context of the contemporary society.

Key words: Conventional boundaries, Mother tongue, Proverbs, Oral literature, Socio-cultural context.

Cultivating Soft Skills Through English Teaching and Learning

— Dr. Ruchika Katiyar

The development of soft skills and personality enhancement are a crucial need of the hour. The students should be made to learn soft skills in order to get an edge over their competitors in the corporate world. Inadequate soft skills produce an unfavourable impact on the employers. English can be considered as a global language and is taught as a second language to the learners. Therefore, it can serve as a medium of imparting the knowledge of ethics, soft skills and human values worldwide because the majority of students face a lacuna of the required skills. The present paper deals with how the soft skills viz. effective communication skills, proficiency in spoken and written language, conversation skills, body language and discussion skills can be cultivated in the students through English teaching and learning.

Keywords: Personality enhancement, ethics, conversation skills, body language

Teaching and Learning English in an ESL Context

— Suneel Prasad

It is generally perceived that English language is taught like a content subject rather than as a skill in most of the educational institutions. The teachers depend on the material to a great extent. They explain and the students are expected to write in the same manner during the exams as a consequence of which the learners are not in a position to exhibit proficiency in communicative abilities. They grope for words in order to speak or write in English. The present paper analyses an ESL classroom as a multidimensional platform entirely open to various interpretations of teaching and learning.

Keywords: Teaching, learning, proficiency, communicative abilities

Achieving Learning Outcomes in English at Primary Level

— Ritika Dabas

Learning outcomes are statements that describe the knowledge or skills, students should acquire by the end of a particular assignment, class,course or programme and help students understand why that knowledge and those skills will be useful to them. Learning outcomes enable teachers to understand learning skills more accurately and effectively provide quality learning experiences in the classrooms and the equal opportunities to all students. The learning outcomes present the benchmark performance level for the children as well as for the teachers, to introspect and correct their pedagogies. Teaching of English in primary classes in India has been a challenge. Achieving class specific learning outcomes becomes furthermore challenging for teaching of English. Use of innovative pedagogies and participatory approach may help teachers to achieve learning outcomes in English at primary level. Maximum exposure to target language helps in gaining command over the language. Developing print rich environment in the classroom wherein teacher places on interesting stories and information on the walls, develops literacy workstations and displays children work on the wall and bulletin boards develops interest for language. Incorporating audio visual aids supporting the textbooks helps in better understanding. Infusing real-life experiences into the instructions enriches classroom learning. including role play in classroom transactions helps children in better communication. Conducting brainstorming sessions on topics of child's interest improves their expression in target language.The present paper attempts to suggest the activities and their pedagogical strategies which the teacher can adapt and adopt to achieve learning outcomes in English for primary classes.

Importance of Soft Skills in English Teaching and Learning

— Miss Chaitra Pandurang Naik

Soft skills are interpersonal skills. They include things like active listening, teamwork, decision making and influencing skills.

Using soft skills in English teaching, which develops the skills of presenting the English lessons a great advantage, since they are normally used in activities such as debating, listening, giving opinions and so on and on the other hand soft skills in the teaching to practice oral and written language efficiently in the English language. Soft skills are the other non-academic skills that students acquire to help them succeed in life. They often include social emotional skills, critical thinking skills and skills, critical thinking skills and skills that facilitate positive interactions with others and the ability to overcome challenges.

Essentially, soft skills refer to both character traits and interpersonal skills that will influence how well a person can work or interact with others. If that sounds a rather large and vague area, that's because it is and the term soft skills covers a wide range of skills as diverse as creativity, time management, problem solving and emotional intelligence.

The Blended Learning and its Impact on English Language Teaching : A Curtain Raiser

— Dr. Soumen Mukherjee

Background

Blended learning is a comparatively newfangled field that syndicates archaic teaching tactics with distance and online gen. The term 'blended learning' actually describes the manner in which eLearning is incorporated or pooled with a more antiquated lecture hall structure, propositioning sovereign study. This particular learning approach warrants that the students remain affianced and their aggregate knowledge becomes prolific. The use of blended learning in the field of English Language Teaching is altogether an innovation in the sense that has been strengthened by the contemporary research that scrutinizes the hypothetical and societal doles of this training gradient. Since it conglomerates customary and online teaching approaches, the assurance of this technique rests on the strengths of both teaching approaches. It is therefore imperative to induct an evaluative charter that deliberates what blended learning fetches to the table for English language acquisition.

Purpose of the Study

This study highlights the prospects offered by blended learning to English language teaching, to find what benefits the method brings to language acquisition. It tries to investigate whether the incorporation of self-paced learning with face-to-face interaction offer any assistance to the participants? Do the efforts worth the rewards? Apart from the target audience, the findings of this study should help teachers at the tertiary level in understanding what exactly to presume from blended learning if they use it as their method of instruction in language learning. At the same time, they must be self-aware of the negative consequences associated with the notion, in order to better inform their decisions.

Methodology

The case study approach was adopted for the research.

Findings

The present review of the literature revealed that blended learning can be used effectively to develop language skills, enhance the English learning environment, and motivate the 21st century's students toward learning the language. With face-to-face teaching and learning, the English teachers can get a wide array of teaching materials and tools that meet the needs of their unique teaching situations. These include texts, audiotapes with accompanying workbooks, videotapes with student worksheets, and various CALL (Computer Assisted Language Learning) programs for teleconferencing and asynchronously or synchronously delivered endeavors, and so on. Some of them are designed for teaching general English while some others are for teaching reading, writing, speaking, listening, grammar, vocabulary-building, cross-cultural communication, pronunciation, English for specific purposes, TOEFL/IELTS preparation, etc.

Future Scope

The application of blended learning does essentially not reject face to face learning, but rather enhance its possibilities. Blended learning — if appropriately conceived developed and delivered — can support any number of learners, anywhere and anytime. Hence, to achieve the learning objectives in the best possible manner, the content developers have to incorporate the technological and other relevant aspects wisely in the learning content. No doubt, there is a dearth of literature that examines the challenges that face language teachers when using blended learning. Therefore, more research has to be done to identify and deal with these challenges.

Key-words: Blended learning; Language acquisition; Training gradient; Application; Challenges.

Disciplining Literature Studies: A Case Study between Banaras Hindu University and Jadavpur University.

— Santanu Das

Abstract: This present paper traces the contrasting attitudes towards the formation of the English syllabus with regards to two institutions in context- Banaras Hindu University and Jadavpur University. Within a comparative analysis, the paper examines how, even as academics engage in ideological thrust and parry with colonization and its fallouts, the epistemological space of English literary studies in the country continues to reflect its colonized character. In Banaras Hindu University, for instance, the English syllabus is never changed/altered to bring in texts that don't necessarily follow the structure of the colonial character. The syllabus is heavy with essays and non-fiction works of British Literature, and has negligible accounts of the same in terms of Indian Literature, that is introduced at the later semesters of the Undergraduate syllabus. In contrast, there is no prioritization in the English syllabus of Jadavpur University, where texts are altered and newer genres introduced at the very beginning, enabling a more wider range in terms of observing literature as a whole. As a result, there is no such structure in the syllabus, and fictional texts and interspersed with cinema, and theatre studies. Through this paper I wish to compare and analyse the approaches of these two Universities in terms of introducing literature in the classroom through a pedagogical format. Having studied in both the Universities, I wish to bring in a mix of personal and objective analysis to interrogate the predicament of institutionalised pedagogical structure in my paper.

How to Collocate Words

— Dr. Yashu Rai

All of us use words in each act of verbal or written communication during a long span of rigorous academic work and even after that. And many of us use words without knowing their exact meaning often. That can prove to be dangerous. A good command over English and word meanings is essential to achieve clarity in language. In fact, this becomes all the more essential when we realise that words are similar but they are absolutely appear to be similar to others in their meaning. And we start making guesses that can get us into trouble.

As English is the second language for us i.e. Indians. It is lethal to operate with assumption while using the language. For what we intend to say might be completely different from what we intend up saying just because we did not check up the dictionary when we learn a language, we learn how individual words combine together in phrases and sentences. Does the following sentence sound right? Meals will be served outside on the terrace, weather allowing. It seems to be an acceptable English sentence and the meaning is not very difficult to understand. They will give us meals outside if the weather is good enough. However it will sound odd to native English speaker. Because the common combination is, in fact, not weather allowing but weather permitting. This is something that a native speaker knows but which we have to learn. It does not help that allow and permit have similar meanings. But only permit is right in this context.

The way in which words belong together as weather and permitting do is known as Collocation.

In order to write and speak natural and correct English, we must know which adjectives are used with certain noun. Your talk, like almost anyone else's is often a flow of words that expresses general reactions and feelings. Tones, gestures and repetitions help you to be clear and understood. But in writing your words are alone. Unless your reader guesses another meaning from the context, your words mean what they say. Get your ideas clear and then choose words to reflect them exactly. Make your sentences make sense.

It is often found that a majority of us have extremely limited awareness of how to collocate words. This not only handicaps our effort to read, write or speak but also greatly discourages learning. In this write up, a comprehensive attempt has been made to learn the meanings of many useful words which are commonly confused by a majority of us; to include as many pairs of words which pose difficulty to us.

Keywords: Collocate; awareness; comprehensive

Inculcating Culture, Soft Skills and Human Values through English Language and Literature

— ***Sunita Sehrawat***

Frank Smith opines "Language is not a genetic gift, it is a social gift. Learning a new language is becoming a member of the club- the community speakers of that language." He further says that "one language sets you in a corridor for life. Two languages open every door along the way." By these two definitions the purpose is to express the importance of a language, other than the mother tongue, for better career opportunities and a better social life. Here the purpose of the author is to share his views on the teaching and learning of English language which is widely spoken across the world and has attained the status of lingua franca. The importance of English language cannot be denied as most of the communication, reading or oral, is carried out in English only. The lack of enthusiasm has been seen among the students for a foreign language as it not spoken in the surroundings. Along with this reluctance of language it has been observed that the soft skills and values among the students do need a great deal of attention. The author in this paper focuses on pointing towards certain indispensible points which if are included in the teaching of English can work manifold and along with an improved language these will help in improving the soft skills and human values in the students.

Creating Sensitivity and Empathy Among Students with the Help of Literature

— Dr. Ajay Kumar

It is rightly said that Literature is the mirror of the society. But, in today's world of internet and social media,children are getting far away from the human virtues like sensitivity and Empathy. With the growing trend of Nuclear families with both the parents working,schools have a greater responsibility in inculcating human values in children and Literatere can play a vital role in developing moral values in children.

Our paper is aimed at developing sensitiveness and Empathy among students of senior classes with the help of the lessons of Literature in vlass XI & XII.We will try to draw some very important and relevant values from the lessons like 'The Ailing Planet', 'Mother's Day', 'The Last Lesson', 'Lost Spring', 'The Rattrap', 'Indigo', 'Journey to the Enf of the Earth', 'Should Wizard Hit Mommy', 'On the Face of It' and 'Memories of Childhood'.

All the above mentioned chapters are epic in themselves and they can teach so many human values that would be helpful for the children in their lives.

We will try to find out the human virtues from these chapters and will include certain stories and examples to make our presentation quite interesting.

Strategies for Teaching First Generation Learners

— Arti Qanungo

This paper is a reflection of my observation and experiences with FIRST GENERATION LEARNERS.

Most of my students are first generation learners and they used to feel uncomfortable with English languageThe hesitant and uncomfortable students felt embarrassed when they are unable to communicate in English.They lacked confidence. When I diagnosed the problem, I found that the issue lay with the pedagogy we employed. We were teaching English the wrong way! We were overseeing the most natural way a child picks up a language: you listen first (at home), speak next, third read and ultimately write. (Listen > Speak > Read > Write). My innovation 'Knock-Knock, Listen To Me' was clearly the need of the situation.

I strongly agree that the students learn better with the help of teaching aids. Audio aids are very much required for the development of listening skills. Although there are constraints of audio aids,that did not stop me from doing so. I used my voice as a resource. I ask my students to listen to my voice with eyes shut, so that only their auditory senses guide them and help them pick up correct enunciation and natural flow of the language.

My students enjoy Knock Knock activity very much. The result was the confidence with which they walk into recital competitions and even managed to win many competitions in the last two years. It makes me extremely proud.

My innovation got international recognition as I was awarded the prestigious title of 'Teacher Innovator of the year 2018' by University of Roehampton, London in collaboration with STIR Education.

Every child is different, every child is unique. So my teaching aids are a wide array of simple and feasible methods suited to the needs of the first generation learners.

To combat the unwillingness of my students to learn, before every lesson, I sensitize my students to the need of the topic in their everyday lives and how it can enable and empower them.

I always involve my students in preparing the teaching aids and the resource material. This develops a student teacher CONNECT and the students also feel proud when they construct anything. They learn by doing.

Inculcating Soft Skills through Teaching of Literature

— ***Neha Anand***

In the midst of the emerging educational trends, malleability in academic courses and mammoth availability of qualified personnels, the competition for job attainment and job sustainability is becoming all the way more strenuous. In order to get an edge over the contenders, students don't have another choice but to add values to their hard skills with soft skills to showcase their prompt caliber across the globe. Numerous researches suggest that Hard skills contribute only 15% in one's success whereas remaining 85% solely depends on soft skills which one possesses. Literature, being mirror to the society, not only entertains but also educates and instructs which delineates the idea of Art for Art's sake and for the society's sake as well. Literature, since ancient times, strongly advocates that literary works should take care of societal welfare and its advancement. The intention of any language is to proffer the learner a life span of contact all the way all the way through the written and spoken expressions. The present paper is an attempt to emphasis on the most important purpose which is, beyond the shadow of doubt, to inculcate soft skills through teaching of Literature. Amid the countless number of literary works accessible in all languages from different societies to us the holy Ramayana, a unique pearl, is an exceptional literary magnum opus with the never-ending relevance and efficacy. This paper focuses on how the eternal and enlightening lighthouse Ramayana is fruitful in cultivating soft skills through its teachings and characters.

Keywords: Literature, Soft Skills, Teaching, Learning, Transformation

Improving Reading Skills of Students of Class Two in English Through Innovative Practices

— Dr. Khaleeq Ahmad, Richa Chahal

The present paper seeks an insight into assessing reading skills of students of class two and adopting innovative practices to improve reading skills. These practices included –

Word wall

Rhyming Words (including jazz chants)

These innovative practices were adopted by the researcher-teacher of English for three months to develop reading skills of the students of class two and to study the implications (of these practices).

Reading assessment tool was discreetly used before and after the study to know the impact of the study. Students were observed in a non-threatening situation through this tool and were placed in any of these categories of readers viz

1. Alphabet Level
2. Word Level
3. Sentence Level

The study was conducted on the premise that in class two in the teaching of English as a second language "students' reading skills were not being enhanced as per the desired outcomes in English and that the skills could be improved by adopting certain innovative practices."

Key words- reading skills, word wall, rhyming words, jazz chants, drilling, sight words, alphabet level, word level, sentence level.

Usage of English Language by Secondary Education Teachers

— *Sonia Behl*

In the last few years there is growing interest in in-service teacher education which aims to help teachers keep up to date with new trends and developments in the field of education. Although this has resulted in upgraded approaches to the design and implementation of teacher training courses which focus main

ly on theoretical and methodological issues neglecting the systematic improvement and development of English teachers' language proficiency and competence. It has been generally seen that government school English teachers feel uncomfortable with using the foreign language inside and outside the classroom. The teachers after teaching students of government schools and using lots of Hindi words in trying to make them understand need to have classes themselves to refresh the language as it is not being used by them outside the class. The present research investigates how comfortable teachers feel with their foreign language proficiency, whether their confidence in using it influences iin anyway their teaching practices and whether there is need for in-service teacher training courses targeting teachers language development and improvement.

From the analysis of the research data we are able to assume that teachers feel that there are deficiencies in their foreign language proficiency and competence and admit that their participation in training courses targeting their language development would improve not only their language proficiency but their actual teaching practices as well. As we have already seen that many practices of letter writing and other such things have changed in the years. We have to keep ourselves updated too. So it is a great practice of revising and learning something new in English in the in-service training which would help the teachers grow and teach better.

Inculcation of Moral Values through English Language

— *Dr. Shalini Sharma*

English is a universal language to express the thoughts and feelings on a common platform. With the help of this single language, anyone can understand others culture, religious concepts, ethics and values very easily because it is hard to have the knowledge of all the languages. Now in this present scenario, the meaning of values and ethics has been changed. None wants to be blind follower or orthodox rather people want to accept the concept that has some logic and facts. They prefer to compare their own principles with other and for this purpose; they are highly interested to study of Bible, Koran and other motivational literature in spite of Ramayana and Gita. It will not be wrong to say that all sort of literature can be analyzed easily by having the knowledge of English language. All religions deal with values relating to human behavior, thinking and action. They teach the real meaning of life and its existence. They prescribe high ethical standards. People should have the knowledge of others customs. Many professional teachers and gurus are making the people fool. They are increasing their business and minting money on account of God and religion. Besides them, some politician parties try to provoke the public at the name of religion. This is only due to the lack of knowledge. All sort of religion cannot be translated in all the languages so this language plays the role of a bridge to connect all the cultures and customs. It helps to understand those hidden points of culture that are beyond the visible-values, beliefs and attitudes. An attempt has been made by this paper how this global language is effective to acquire some essential moral values by various activities and the main focus of this paper is connected with inculcation of values.

Key Words- Inculcation, scenario, orthodox, ethical standards, prescribe.

Classroom 2.0: Incorporating ICT and Theatre for an Effective Learning Environment for ESL

— *Srishti Gupta*

Language acquisition in the early years stems from mimicking one's environment. A conscious study of language can be an interesting as well as a harrowing experience for students, especially when it comes to English, because of the pressure to 'improve English' a misnomer students often use. Recently there have been two major changes in the curriculum of Functional English at Delhi University, the introduction of a compulsory module on communicative English and application-based evaluation of language skills. This paper originates from my experience of teaching these papers to girl-students in the Sunday Teaching Centre. Some of these students were first-generation English learners.

To engage the diverse cohort. I used some non-traditional methods of teaching.

The main focus of my paper lies in presenting the classroom activities improvisation exercises, Spin-A-Yarn and so on, that form an essential part of my pedagogy. These activities perform the role of bridging the gap between the traditional classrooms and the college coursework, the prerequisite for which is original thinking. They have been used during classroom sessions as well as for assessment. They also complement the changes in the curriculum and would prove useful pedagogical tools for ELT at Delhi University. They can be used as a means of continuous informal evaluation.

These activities incorporate theatre and tapping the potential of ICT and help with various aspects of language teaching, from grammar and reading to speaking and listening skills. I argue that adapting the pedagogical tools to the things that interest them on the internet, like vines, memes, stand-up comedy and so on increases the effectivity of language learning. This is achieved by the role process-oriented learning plays in facilitating the students to overcome the anxiety of language learning. Finally, I also comment on how various transversal skills are transferred in the process

Multilingual Norms for Assessing Speaking Skills of Adult Learners

— Dr. Tulika Prasad

The paper is based on a research study that aims to incorporate multilingual (ML) norms to assess speaking skills of adult learners as part of a proficiency test. It argues that ML norms need to be used especially at lower levels of language proficiency in an ESL (English as a second language) context. This is not only because the adult learner is unable to use L2 effectively for communication, but also because, in the process of acquiring L2 using his/her L1 resources, the learner is able to use two or more languages almost simultaneously to communicate and therefore acquires the ability to wield those languages more effectively. The research study attempts to develop test tasks and ML norms for assessment that acknowledge the learners' L1 proficiency in speaking in unseen contexts and thus tries to lend legitimacy to an adult learner's use of L1 to support communication in L2 in ML contexts.

The study draws on researchers' experience of being teachers of language and literature and more recently of the English Language Proficiency Course at the University of Delhi where the language proficiency of adult learners is assessed in all the four skills. Data from test performance on the speaking tests as well as reported data from students, teachers, examiners of speaking tests of international boards (IELTS and GESE) and ELT experts is analyzed to arrive at a valid and reliable assessment scheme that uses communicative test tasks and assessment criteria that incorporate ML norms. The paper will present examples of data to illustrate the convergence of views of different stakeholders and the theoretical framework arrived at in terms of the types of speaking tasks and the rubrics.

Keywords: multilingual norms, validity, adult learner

Some Innovative Practices in Teaching & Learning of English at Secondary Level

—Asha Khurana

The Researcher has been teaching English at secondary level in different schools of Delhi government for past twenty five years and would like to share some of the classroom practices which resulted in better learning and generated interest in students.

During this tenure and also currently, the researcher involves the students into five minute mindfulness practice in a language learning class. Further, at times to relieve their boredom, stress caused by previous heavy classes and to control their distracted mind they are made to practice AANA PAANA breathing technique of vippassana for 3 to 5 minutes. This results in focus, concentration and calmness of mind hence better learning.

For vocabulary building:

The researchers introduces proverbs and phrasal verbs, regularly for few days ,and then they are asked to weave them into narratives, they come up with many funny narratives which bring laughter and smile on all the faces in the class.

Textbook lessons are taught highlighting all new words. After completion of few lessons, randomly words are asked : from which lesson and in what context it is used in the lesson and later question goes like: can you use the word in your own sentence?

The researcher would like to illustrate and share her experinces while teaching students through Graphic Organisers, Venn Diagram, Frayer Model, Foldables and like. Apart from these newspaper reports, advertisements, articles are used to taught the sub skills of writing as a process.

Three Day UGC Sponsored International Seminar and Workshop On "Innovative Teaching, Learning and Evaluation in English: Harmonious Transition from School to University" – A Report

Day 1 (January 23rd, 2020)

The first day of the Three day UGC Sponsored seminar titled "Innovative Teaching, Learning and Evaluation in English: Harmonious Transition from School to University" witnessed a footfall of young researchers, scholars, professors, teachers and students. The topic was well received by the audience attending the seminar. The seminar and workshop's proceedings are as written below.

Introductory Remarks and Welcome Address

The seminar began with a musical session performed by the Music Department of the college. The Head of the English Department, Dr. Ruchi Mundeja introduced and felicitated all the guests and speakers for the ensuing session. The Principal of the college, Dr. Pratyush Vatsala delivered an introductory speech on the status of the English language as practically the lingua franca of India and its use as medium of communication for teaching and learning in educational institutions. She pointed out how Indian culture has advantageously utilised every crisis it has faced. She thus highlighted the utilisation of English as a privilege in terms of a benefit of colonization.

SESSION I: Curriculum Framework (A Global Perspective)

Inaugural Address by Dr. Kavita Sharma

Dr. Kavita Sharma (Former President, South Asian University) delivered the inaugural address wherein she critiqued the "functional English" taught in schools in India which merely equips students to speak the language but not to articulate arguments cogently. She adopted a contrary position in stating that as "a legacy of colonization" English is the only language that we are left with as a common means of communication in a multilingual country such as ours. But it amounts to a status symbol. She did not argue for the eradication of English but lamented the lack of "aptitude assessment" and "language competencies". Dr. Kavita Sharma argued that there is no communication between secondary school teachers and college teachers in India. In High School teaching high scores are the concern whereas college curriculum requires critical thinking and analysing. In schools there is no counselling and there is lack of rigour. According to her board exams stultify growth and should be got rid of. English is often the language of upward mobility and globalisation.

Keynote Address by Professor C. B. Sharma

In a different vein, Prof. C. B. Sharma (Chairman, NIOS) argued that during the transition from school to university, mere language studies in school isn't insufficient. He also questioned why Vedas were not being studied. According to him, even though fifty percent Indians know Hindi, English is privileged. He therefore insists on the use of English only along with Indian languages. Prof. C. B. Sharma invoked Macaulay on how he introduced English to rule India for a longer time and how we have still not been able to rid ourselves of this influence. As per Sharma, English should be taught in India but the content should be Indian. For example, Vedic education should be imparted in English language.

Address by Chief Guest Vineet Joshi

Mr. Vineet Joshi (IAS, Director General of NTA), privileged the Nation above the individual student. He advocates the Continuous and Comprehensive Evaluation that he introduced at the school level so that students can assess themselves instead of focusing entirely on end-semester exams. He argues in favour of assessing speaking and listening skills in colleges as he and others had introduced in schools. Mr. Joshi expressed concern over disappearing regional languages. In standing up for regional languages, an important concern is to connect the classroom to the outside world. He argued for creative, critical thinking abilities to be cultivated.

Address by Professor Kapil Kapoor

Prof. Kapil Kapoor (Chairman, IIAS) established English as "an unscientific language". He contrasted that with Indian languages as comprising of "intellect, memory and application". Drawing upon the rich Indian linguistic heritage, Prof. Kapoor highlighted the need to revisit the works of Native scholars and theorists such as Patanjali, Panini etc. He further favours the moral aspect of language as meaningful or wasteful. Criticising language learning in Indian schools as divided between mechanical multiple choices, which teach how to speak without expressing, he insists on the differentiation of language as "compositional or spoken". He stressed on focusing upon the syntactical and semantic aspects of language studies while arguing for a more holistic and engaging approach language learning and teaching.

SESSION II: Relevance of Contextualized Context

Major Harsh Kumar (Secretary, NCERT) opened this session. He adopted a liberal humanistic approach towards education and rather than "algebra, Marx and Lenin" he stresses on understanding oneself through education. For him education is about transforming one's personality in order to behave rightly in societal relationships. Knowledge has to be converted to "wisdom".

Major Kumar's address was followed by Prof. Sandhya Sahoo (English, NCERT). Her argument was that language cannot be learned, it has to be acquired. Due to this, in NCERT, their approach is interdisciplinary and multilingual. The materials used for teaching are composite and integrated with the context. She emphasized on the need to learn written language like spoken mother tongue is, offering stories first to students and then specific words.

SESSION III: Innovative Teaching and Learning Pedagogies in English

This session began with an Address by Dr. Elaine Boyd (Associate Academic, University College, London). In her address Dr Boyd revisited the ideas around 21st Century language skills (Communication, Collaboration, creativity and Critical Thinking) and tested their relevance against the changing times of mechanistic labour and employment. She argued for changing the discourse of ELS (English Literary Skills) from "what" is taught to "how" it's taught. Dr. Boyd revaluated these four central pillars and provided points towards their redefinitions. Communication skills should be judged not just based on grammar competency but also for their content. This shall result in building their creative capacities while providing them the opportunity to become critical self-learners, who shall also become adept at genuine collaboration rather than just its functional use. She ended her presentation by asking all to reconcile contemporary educational pedagogies with the principles of self reliance.

Dr. Boyd was followed by a riveting address from Dr. Geeta Rai (Assistant Professor at CIE, University of Delhi). Dr. Rai interrogated the need and possibilities of innovation within language studies and skill development. She critiqued traditional methodologies of overcrowded classroom driven by unidirectional flow of information. Dr. Rai further made the case for reinventing evaluation strategies for modern learners by focusing more on praxis and less on theory. She developed this point by outlining Bloom's taxonomical table: Remember – Understand – Apply – Analyze – Evaluate – Create. She closed her address by examining the example of Khan Academy as a new possibility within modern education and teaching.

SESSION IV: Innovative Practices for Teaching first Generation Learners

The last session for the day comprised of one presentation delivered by Dr. Prerna Malhotra (Assistant Professor at RLA College, University of Delhi) and two presentations from Mr. Amit Sharma and Mr. Pradeep Sharma. In her presentation, Dr. Malhotra highlighted the impediments affecting first generation learner of English such as the lack of parental help and the absence of the educational connection between parents and teachers. Treating English as simply a language, she further asked teachers to focus on knowledge bank of languages rather than thinking of them as technical skills. Her argument focused on performance oriented learning, making the same an integral part of educators ethical responsibility.

Mr. Amit Sharma in his paper shed light on his experience as a Teach For India fellow to talk about how the usage of carefully constructed literary tools, such as Visualization and Sensory Stimulation Learning Theory, help students develop a sense of experiential learning. He talked about some of the methodologies he had used to create an immersive classroom environment for his students to help them develop and sustain an interest in learning, pointing how visualization helps children in improving their basic grasp on concepts, learning new words, and helps them explore themes deeply. He further argued that literature, when coupled with immersive pedagogy (such as sing-along lessons, play-acting, directed conversations in peer groups, etc.), can help strengthen techniques meant to increase classroom literacy levels that are often challenged by socio-economic factors the children face.

Mr. Pradeep Sharma in his presentation brought forth the growing need for common language i.e. English in the globalized economy and the standardization of language proficiency to meet global standards. He highlighted how until there is a standardized approach, proficiency building is a farfetched goal. He also explored Common European Reference of Languages: Learning, Teaching and Assessment, as a frame to describe achievements of foreign learners. Mr. Sharma also questioned if standardization would be feasible for institutions (school /college) in rural areas due to lack of trained teachers from the researcher's long experience of imparting English language teaching.

Day 2 (January 24th, 2020)

SESSION I: Overview of Assessment/Evaluation By Experts From Trinity College London, India With Special Reference To UGC Evaluation Reforms

The second day of the International Seminar and Workshop began with a session conducted by Dr. Elaine Boyd. According to Dr. Boyd, the challenge for teachers' lies in finding out how each student is learning, identify the gaps in learning and use the information to close that gap. If individual learning issue is not addressed at the primary level, it leads to even bigger gap in learning as the students go higher in school. Dr. Boyd enumerated 7 Principles to use which will ensure that all students in a classroom are included in the learning process, which are as follows:

The Teacher Mindset: How mistakes and errors are assessed and reviewed in classrooms.

Power of Question: Asking the right questions and focusing not on the quantity but the quality of the questions.

Tyranny of the Task: Shift in pedagogy, where task-based activities are emphasized over text based exercises.

Cold Calling: All students should be involved in teacher - student dialogue, with time to think.

No Opt Out: Teachers must ensure a safe environment where students are allowed to make mistakes without being reprimanded.

Whole Class Response: Focus should not be on who got the question right, but on how a teacher responds to individual learning capacity of the students.

Deep Checking: Assessment to check whether students have really reached the level of understanding the teacher has been aiming for.

Say it Again Better: Allowing students to rephrase or fully form their answers by asking them the same questions again and again.

Reduce Scaffolding: As this results in giving students a sense of having completed a task without actually learning.

Mrs. Neelima Sharma followed Dr. Boyd with her presentation in which she attempted to facilitate her role as an information transfer on NEP, what it entails, its objectives and the role of learning outcome. Students have various challenges in life which would involve learning life skills related to dealing with life issues like anger, failure and disappointments. Students need to be taught on learning to live in a multicultural society and mediate between different cultures globally as well.

SESSION II: Innovative Approaches to Assessments

Ms. Alka Rai (Ex-HOD English, Air Force Golden Jubliee Institute) began this session and talked about the need to question the process of teaching and learning in order to discern where in lies the problem of gap in learning. She reiterated the need to include exercise in critical thinking in classrooms and also to place strong emphasis on developing listening skills in students. She argued how we need to accept and adopt parameters of assessment according to the needs of the students. She argued how while assessing a creative paper, the focus should be the student's creativity. There are other platforms to check the grammar and syntax skills.

Mr. Khaleed Ahmeed (Principal, DOE) presented his finding on his research on "Improving Reading Skills of Class II in English through Innovative Practices." There were various responses to his question on how to improve reading skills of students which include watching English movies with subtitles, reading newspapers, reading something interesting and short, watching songs with lyrics, making list of words etc. Responding to questions regarding absentee students and overburdened syllabi, Mr. Ahmeed highlighted how there is no formal evaluation for students till grade V, asking teachers to focus on the learning rather than covering syllabus.

Talks by Ms. Alka Rai and Mr. Khaleed Ahmeed were followed by four paper presentations which are briefly outlined below:

Ms. Asha Khurana utilized her 25 years of active classroom experience to argue how mindfulness practice in a language learning class can help relieve their boredom, stress caused by previous heavy classes and to control students distracted; using practices such as AANA PAANA breathing technique of vippassana for 3 to 5 minutes.

Using educational statistics collected from Budgam, Kashmir, Ms. Nayeema highlighted how progressive improvement played a key role in the learning of English language. She outlined how innovative curriculum, early focus on language skills and vernacular medium up to middle school level can further facilitate educational pedagogies across language studies.

Ms. Nidhi Pradeep in her presentation highlighted the need to define goals based on action oriented proficiency level measurement instead of current achievement oriented ones based on quantitative grading. Accordingly, this would leave greater room for innovations for teachers and educators.

Dr. Valaria analyzed approaches to English language teaching (in terms of curriculum, materials, etc.) in view of the changes in the perception of the role of English. Delving into the changing form and the status of English, her paper scrutinized approaches to English language teaching and learning.

SESSION III: Innovative Approaches to Assessments

Dr. Sanjay Verma was the first speaker in the third session. The focus of his talk was on assessments. With the help of the parable "An Animal School" he raises questions on the current assessment system in education and also pointed out the problems in current education and assessment process. According to him, in our society, learning is over emphasized and directionless. Contemporary education is not application based; it is tilted towards acquiring information. Learning is a process of fulfilment but our school education systems are not allowing this to happen, instead we are producing a muddled generation who want to make money but don't have communication skills and a command on language.

Dr. Neelam Kulshrestha's (PGT English, DOE) address followed Dr. Verma's presentation. As per Dr Kulshrestha today most of the teachers are teaching what they learnt 20-30 years ago. There is a need to innovate new teaching techniques and skills in our education system. New assessment tools should be initiated. It's a duty of a teachers to know the level of theirs students learning they should guide the students and motivate the students in learning. She emphasized on the overall grooming of the students. According to het, obtaining good marks should not be the only criteria of success. She discussed government project "BUNIYAD" through which govt has initiated the policy to educate each and every child in holistic manner.

The session was then carried forward with paper presentation outlined below:

Ms. Vandana in her research paper studied language patterns of five teacher educators. A major finding within her study was how language patterns could determine the state of happiness of a mind with reliable precision. Her study indicated that language plays a very important and significant role in creating a state of happiness.

Dr. Ruchika Katiyar engaged with student's capacity to learn soft skills in order to get them an edge over their competitors, highlighting how inadequate soft skills produce an unfavorable impact on the employers. She further highlighted how soft skills viz. effective communication and conversation skills, body language and discussion skills can be cultivated in students through English teaching and learning.

Ms. Garima Bhatnagar in her paper compared elements of language from the works of Noam Chomsky and Panini, their treatment of linguistic elements and approach towards language. She further compared Chomsky's definitions for the structure and function of all languages against Panini's attempt to anthologize the working of the language of his time.

Dr. Meena explored how the study of proverbs can help lend an element of interest and bonding to English studies. Furthermore, she highlighted how the study of proverbs can reveal themselves as forms of resistance culture and inherited wisdom.

SESSION IV: Discussion on Feasibility and Replicability of Evaluation Strategy

The final address for the second day of the seminar was delivered by Dr. Mukti Sanyal (Officiating Principal at Bharti College, University of Delhi) who delved upon the purpose, function and meaning of student evaluation. Bringing to limelight how contemporary educational structures focus on evaluation as simply a strategy of scoring students and inflating marks, Dr. Sanyal asks her audience to rethink the direction for evaluation to cater to the multipurpose needs of the new generation of learners. She ended her presentation outlining evaluation as a strategy of monitoring and mentoring student progress rather than quantifying and scoring their skills.

Dr. Sanyal's address was followed by brief paper presentation outlined below:

Mr. Yashu Rai in his presentation focused upon the difference between written and spoken English. He made the case for a rigorous and thorough exercise for the mastery of English as a written language, highlighting how language script requires clarity of meaning and intention, which can otherwise be negotiated while speaking.

Ms. Srishti Gupta argued how adapting pedagogical tools to the things that interest students, such as the internet, vines, memes, stand-up comedy etc. can increases the affectivity of language learning. She also focused on how various transversal skills are transferred through this process.

Ms. Smriti Ashra in her paper focused on how teachers can make learning easy, fun and long lasting for the learners who are curious yet confused but can find the direction of their interest when supported with proper guidance, efficient teacher and effective support of audio visual technology.

Ms. Swasti Sharma focused upon cinematic adaptation as a pedagogy that links school/ university acquired knowledge to the lived experiences of students. The focal point of her paper was a close textual /trans-textual analysis of the innovative approaches adopted by contemporary academics in ESL/EFL countries for the study of not just the English language and literature.

Ms. Sonia Bhel in her research investigates how comfortable teachers were with foreign language proficiency. She illustrated how teachers felt that there were deficiencies in foreign language proficiency and agreed on how their participation in training courses targeting language development would improve their language proficiency and teaching practices.

Day 3 (January 25th, 2020)

SESSION I: Live Demonstrations of Assessments and Washback effect by Trinity College London

Dr. Boyd started her paper on classroom assessment by raising the question of who should be involved in classroom assessment. She says that usually the teacher decides how the assessment should be done and children are often not involved in the process. She emphasized the involvement of students in classroom assessment. This called for allowing errors and experimentation and risk taking in the class room. Dr. Boyd introduced the MARGE Principle of learning, MARGE being the acronym for five essential principles of learning: Motivate, Attend, Relate, Generate, and Evaluate. She also presented seven class room exercises that will help in making classroom assessment fun, interactive and efficient.

Mrs. Neelima Sharma started her presentation with a definition of summative assessment and differentiating it from formative assessment. She says that summative assessment has a Washback effect and it affects class room environment. Videos of GESE test for Grade 2 and Grade 5 conducted by Trinity College was shown which was followed by a discussion on the method of test that was shown in the video. After an interactive time of discussion, Mrs. Neelima gave an overview of the method of oral assessment that was shown in the video.

SESSION II: Synthesizing of the Insights and Compiling of Reports to prepare a Guideline or Reference Manual for Teachers of English

Dr. Vinod Kumar Singh (Assistant Professor at Department of English, University of Delhi) spoke on the topic "Relevance and Efficacy of Higher Education Reforms in Higher Education". He traced the history of English studies in India from the colonial times to the present time. Dr. Singh looked at what he deemed to be the failures and gaps in the National Education Policies that have been implemented in India over the decades. He spoke a little bit about the NEP introduced recently and made an observation that it a move in the right direction while noting that anything new comes with its own challenges.

Dr. Sharavan Kumar, who followed Dr. Singh's presentation, spoke on the topic CALL (Computer-assisted Language Learning) to MALL (Mobile Assisted Language Learning). He looked at the meaning of learning and teaching in the age of technology. He emphasize that teachers are actually facilitators. Dr. Shravan introduced many tools offered by mobile phones and internet that can be used in the classroom.

VALEDICTORY SESSION: Presentation of the First draft of the Synthesized Report (Findings and Conclusions)

This session comprised of an exhaustive and elaborate presentation made by esteemed Principal Dr. Pratyush Vatsala. She introduced certain foundational tenets of the upcoming alternative educational format of Bhartia Shiksha Board (BSB), with special reference to the role of linguistic and language studies within the same. She expounded upon the central ideas underpinning this new format of education as a merger between traditional structures of Indian educational pedagogies with western modalities of learning and teaching. Dr. Vatsala highlighted how this new structure will focus on the holistic development of students, taking into account their physical, intellectual, emotional as well as spiritual needs while also accommodating sustainable developmental goals and objectives.

Targeting to expand education beyond its materialist boundaries, Dr. Vatsala showcased how this new venture shall strike a critical balance between the economic and academic purposes of education. Herein the role of language studies and literature will prove itself indispensible. Through the example of Grade II syllabus under the proposed new syllabi for BSB, Dr. Vatsala outlined how the course shall combine texts from a diverse array of cultures and their literatures. She went to tentatively draw out the structure as comprising 10 percent of translated Ancient Indian Texts, 40 percent of Indian Literatures (sourced from cross the length and breadth of the country, inclusive of Indian diversity in all its forms) and 50 percent of International Literatures (reflecting a multitudes of cultural and social spaces). She also stressed upon the fact that assessment under this new Board shall move beyond quantitative analysis and equally focus upon the qualitative grasp of students over the theoretical and practical aspects of the syllabus. This shall be achieved through an invigorating series of external and internal assessments that shall essentially remain holistic and flexible.

VOTE OF THANKS: The Department of English Faculty

The valedictory session marked the conclusion of the three day International Seminar and Workshop. The closing speech delivered by senior faculty members of the Department of English provided a fitting closure to the event. Extending her gratitude to the various esteemed panelists and speakers, Dr. Sucheta Chaturvedi gratefully recognized the contributions made by each and every speaker to the discourse on silence and its many tangents. Furthermore, acknowledging the many hours of tireless work and efforts put into making this conference a success, and extended her heartfelt gratitude to the faculty members of the Department of English and the wide network of non teaching technical and administrative staff, without which the conference could not have taken place. Dr. Chaturvedi additionally made the case of freeing education and all its facets from partisan political ideologies and to reorient language studies to both its features, written and oral, rather than simply continuing on the same as a field of technical skill.

Dr. Chaturvedi's address was followed by Ms. Anju Dahiya who congratulated everyone present for their contribution to the ideas explored across the three days of the seminar and workshop. She further commented how everyone present has been provided with both, personal and professional opportunities, to enrich their academic lives. Ms. Deeba Zafir then delivered her address, highlighting how the event has allowed one and all to partake in the processes of reinvigorating our educational infrastructure and ended on the note of continuing forth with the love of learning.

The final address concluding the event was delivered by Dr. Ruchi Mundeja. She extended her praise to the hard work of student volunteers of the English Department. She delved into integral aspects arising out of the conference and highlighted how administrative and bureaucratic blockades continue to be the greatest challenge to learning and educational pedagogies. Furthermore, Dr. Mundeja highlighted the need of the hour, that is, to listen to our students and learners with due diligence and respect, which in turn will allow teachers and educators alike to further the cause of education. She closed her speech by asking all present to carry forth the ideas and debates born out the three days of scintillating and rigorous academic engagement into our daily lives.

Technical Committee
Brijesh, Meenakshi & Dolly

List of Contributors

Srishti Gupta - Guest Lecturer in English, University of Delhi.

Harpreet Kaur - Children's Author, Founder: Jumpstart Spoken English Program, ELT Resource Person to NCERT & SCERT.

Dr. Yashu Rai - Associate Professor, Department of English, D. N. College, Hisar.

Garima Bhayana - Research Scholar, Chaudhary Bansi Lal University, Bhiwani.

Amit Sharma - Lakshmibai College, University of Delhi.

Dr. Meena Sehrawat - Senior Lecturer, DIET Ghumanhera, SCERT Delhi.

Dr. Khaleeq Ahmad - Directorate of Education, New Delhi.

Richa Chahal - Directorate of Education, New Delhi.

Sunita Sehrawat - Research Scholar, K R Mangalam University.

Garima Bhatnagar - DOE, NCT of Delhi.

Malvika Oberoi - Department of English, R.B.S, Rewari (Haryana).

Nidhi Pradeep Sharma - Research Scholar, Department of English & CLS, Saurashtra University, Rajkot, Gujarat (India).

Arti Qanungo - TGT English, GGSSS School Block, Shakarpur, Directorate of Education, Nct Delhi.

Asha Khurana - Lecturer in English, The School of Excellence, Dwarka.

Pradeep Sharma - English Learning Studio, Jamnagar, Gujarat (India).